The Cookie Jar of Life

Dorothy L. Hansen

Copyright © 2013 Dorothy L. Hansen
All rights reserved

ISBN: 978-0-615-91240-0

Library of Congress Control Number: 2014900278

The Cookie Jar in the photograph on the cover was made by Joseph Mast and given to the Hansen Family by Joseph and Marion Mast, who were good friends and neighbors in the early 1960s.

The image of the ℏ ending each story was designed by Bob Hansen originally for the monogram on the family silverware, a wedding gift from his parents.

I dedicate this book to all those
who believe in and strive for peace in the world.

The book you hold in your hands would not have been made possible without the support of my many dear friends and family members. I give special thanks to my writing teacher, Suzanne Sherman, for her encouragement over the years and assistance with selecting the stories for my book. I also thank my daughter-in-law Robyn for help with proof reading and locating all the photos for my stories and son Tom for scanning and formatting them, but most of all, I am grateful for their dedication to making sure a dream of mine came true.

Contents

PROLOGUE: THE PERFECT SETTING FOR MY MEMOIR'S VIII

PART ONE: MY EARLY YEARS 1

A RICH LITTLE POOR GIRL 3
BYE-LO BABY: CHRISTMAS 1927 7
THE BLUE DIARY 11
MY SISTER ANN 15
SUMMERTIME IN THE COUNTRY 21
THE SUMMER OF LOVE 25
PAT'S WEDDING 29
GINGERSNAPS 33
MISS MARJORIE STAFFORD 35
TWO YOUNG MEN 37

PART TWO: MY LATER EARLY YEARS 41

HEY ROMEO 43
OH, HAPPY, HAPPY WEDDING DAY 47
A UNIQUE MIND 51
THE LOT MAN 55
THE ORIGINAL CALIFORNIA KOOK 59
HABITATS FOR THE HANSENS 61
LIFE AFTER DEATH 63
FIRSTBORN SON 67
JULIA'S PREDICAMENT 71
THIRD TIME'S THE CHARM: HERE COMES TOM 73
PAUL DAVID HANSEN IS BORN 77
TIME FOR MISCHIEF 81
THE SHINNY POLE 83
GENESIS OF R&D PRODUCTS, INC. 85
EYE OF A NEEDLE 89
THE SIX-LEGGED COW 93
PRESERVING THE LEGACY 95
THE CARD 97

PART THREE: MY LATER YEARS ... 99

- AN INTERVIEW WITH ME AT 84 ... 101
- VISIONS ... 105
- OUR FIRST GRANDCHILD IS BORN ... 107
- DEAR ALICIA ... 113
- NEW DIMENSIONS ... 115
- AN HOUR OF SUNSHINE ... 119
- AN EMBARRASSING EVENT ... 121
- BETTER THAN A HALLMARK ... 123
- CHICKEN MARBELLA ... 125
- CHOCOLATES AND BIRDSEED ... 127
- SEAT 21E ... 129
- CHRISSY AND THE SAUERKRAUT SORORITY ... 133
- DEALING WITH FEAR ... 137
- $36.10 DOWN THE DRAIN ... 139
- A FLOWER IN THE WRONG PLACE ... 141
- GRAY DAZE ... 143
- PAT AND THE PICKLES ... 145
- WHERE'S THE BEACH BALL? ... 147
- THOMAS' ETAL ... 151
- LETTERS ... 153
- MY GUEST TOWEL DILEMMA ... 155
- REMARKS FOR JACK RUDINOW'S MEMORIAL SERVICE ... 157
- JACKSON ... 159
- LOVE, SWEET LOVE ... 161
- STAYING FOCUSED ... 165
- TEACHING VALUES ... 167
- CONNECTIONS ... 169
- A PERFECT DAY ... 171
- A QUIET PLACE ... 173
- A VERSION OF THROWING OUT THE BABY WITH THE BATH WATER ... 175
- MY POST OFFICE ADMIRER ... 177
- THOUGHTS ABOUT DYING ... 179

PART FOUR: ON POLITICS ... 183

- LETTER TO PRESIDENTIAL CANDIDATE JOHN KERRY ... 185
- DIFFERENT PERSPECTIVES ... 187
- ABU GHRAIB ... 189
- LETTER TO AN ELDERLY IRAQI WIDOW ... 191
- HARD WORK ... 193

HEY, HEY, HO, HO, WTO HAS GOT TO GO 195
LETTER TO THE IRS 197
TAX POLICY AND THE UNION HOTEL 199
NOTICE OF DEFICIENCY... 201
WHY I DIDN'T FILE A 2002 TAX RETURN 203
WHAT WILL I DO? 205
THE GIANT UMBRELLA 207
BUT WHAT DID I DO? 211

PART FIVE: POETRY 213

THE MIDNIGHT CALLER 221
FOR TEDDY 223
ON AGING.. 225
A POLKA DOT PATH 227
A BUMP ON THE HEAD... 229
BEACONS OF LIGHT AROUND THE WORLD 231
I LOVE YOU, ROBYN 233
THE REMINDER OF MY GOOD FORTUNE 235

Dorothy's patio, Wilton Ave, Sebastopol, CA. circa 2011

PROLOGUE: THE PERFECT SETTING FOR MY MEMOIR'S

When you think of the societal good performed by authors of memoirs: it's therapeutic, it keeps old folks off the streets, that sort of thing - it makes one want to write one's own life story, and to write so well it could be published.

In my case, I aim to write only for my family's consumption, which somewhat limits the damage I'll create as I have only 103 living family members...so far. I hope, with dedicated practice, to improve my skills, but I wonder if I have the right setting to inspire brilliant, creative truth telling.

I'm sitting at the computer desk in my overstuffed bedroom/office in my apartment on Wilton Street in Sebastopol feeling a little hemmed in by the storage boxes surrounding me. (I can't sort them out as I'm too busy accumulating new stuff to store.) Swiveling around in my chair, I see that I've used space wisely: I've left a crooked path to the clothes closet leaving not quite enough room for the copier/fax/scanner (which only slightly interferes with opening the closet door); the c/f/s abuts my paper-cluttered desk which I know is there although I can't actually see it. Turning more to my left, there's a seven-shelf Ikea bookshelf, then the bed that has under it three nice big drawers, two of which I can open...the third hits the desk leg if I open it just a few inches. I can get my hand in enough to retrieve whatever I put there before the desk got in the way. I could go around the rest of the room, but you get the idea...another Ikea bookshelf, a chest of drawers with original husband-designed-and-constructed storage shelves consuming space to the ceiling. And that monstrous five-drawer Allsteel khaki-colored file cabinet which my late friend Glenda advised me years ago to give to Goodwill or "For God's sake, Dodo, give it a coat of paint!"

It embarrasses me to tell you that my husband and I owned a business to manufacture and distribute products that Bob invented, unique products designed to organize papers. Message holders to hold phone messages where you can't miss them; file card holders that leave space when you retrieve a card so you can easily put it back right where it belongs; copyholders, without annoying clips, that hold what you were copying upright, to hold it in place; curved Perky wall pockets to hold paper and magazines upright so they don't slump over. Working with these products should have infused me with a sense of orderliness.

But I'm the kind of person who, after typing a proper recipe card from a friend's scribbled notes, will keep the scribbling to help me remember my friend just the way she is. As I make turns in my swivel chair, I look at the woven basket Jack and Linda brought me from Tuvalu and think of them and their good work with Save the Children; I marvel at the perfect, intricate, geometric sculptures made of colorful cardboard and paste and inspired by Islamic art that my friend Nina Cohen gave to me; I breathe more freely as I feel the openness of the imagined desert scene in Florence Dixon's painting above my bed: the basket of clean unfolded clothes won't let me forget that neglected task; the brown velour folding knitting pouch reminds me of the one good thing about working at OCLI (Optical Coating Laboratories) for five years. The pouch was given to me as a thank you for initiating an employees' credit union.

There on the wall, in its pristine beauty, is a two-column display of Perky pockets holding The Progressive, Friends Bulletin, The Objector, The Sun, Mother Jones, and Sunset, each held upright without ever a drooping corner.

And there's the framed black and white wedding photo. Bob and I look so much in love. Now, alone in my crowded little room, sweet memories of him encourage me...and give purpose to my writing. Sitting here, with the morning sun filtered through the blinds, hearing the voices of my neighbors as they exchange ordinary, everyday, caring-about-you greetings, I wonder what kinds of stories I will tell. Is this the space for me to write from the heart so my family will know not just the names and dates but the feelings and hopes and dreams of those who are their heritage. Is this where I can learn to write well enough so they will want to read the words I put on paper? Or, will I produce writing like that on the large sculpture in the foyer of the Di Rosa Preserve in Napa? An artist has created a form perhaps fifteen feet high consisting of large boxes, like manila-colored shipping cartons sized to hold TVs or microwaves, stacked loosely crosshatched one on top of another. On each box in large block letters is written one word. The viewer beholds, as his eye travels upwards, some 15 feet of nothing but BLAH, BLAH, BLAH, BLAH, BLAH, BLAH, BLAH, BLAH, BLAH, BLAH.

The elitist who wrote that it's sad so many memoirs are printed might, instead, give thought to some of the authentically sad things happening in our world today. A published memoir might help a violated person to reject revenge, an abused person to leave an untenable situation, a young person to refuse to kill for empire, a congressperson to say no to corporate bribes, or a president to honor the rule of law. A memoir, written with the pen and from the heart of any person, contributes to our common history and knowledge of ourselves and our world. Each person's life history has standing. Rather than grieve over the number in print, every memoir should be celebrated and cherished. I can't foretell how well I will succeed in writing stories that my family will want to read, but for me, now, I find much pleasure in spending time at the computer in my comfortably-cluttered bedroom/office with freedom to write what I please and power to delete at will.

If I ever finish my book and a publisher should find it irresistible and if it is printed and available to the public, I might find new pleasure in sharing memories of my family with others.

I think I'll stick with the comfort of my present writing room. It may not be the perfect setting, but it seems to fit my style. Do you think it would be unbecoming to call it my "writing studio"...that is, when I'm a published writer?

PART ONE: MY EARLY YEARS

A RICH LITTLE POOR GIRL

Oklahoma was one of the first states to experience the Great Depression, even before the stock market crash in 1929, and it hit our family hard. But the sheltering arms of family protected me from the grim realities my parents faced as they struggled to keep their big family fed and sheltered and many years passed before I fully understood how desperately poor we were when we moved to Norman in 1928. My memories are of happy growing-up times, especially with Mary.

Daddy owned the Sunshine Mercantile Company in Duncan, Oklahoma, a successful enterprise which supported his growing family in some style. The Lockett family was well respected in the community. They lived in a nice house and were one of the few families that owned a car. Mother was a member of a women's literary society, and the children were honored at school for good grades and good citizenship.

Sunshine Mercantile, Walter Lockett on left, circa 1928

Susan Alberta Ivins Patty

Walter Melancthon Lockett

There are family snapshots of my parents with their well-dressed children: Walter, Susan Patty, Lloyd, and Mary—attending family picnics, and there are formal photographs of them as well. Not long after I was born in 1920, the financial picture changed for the Lockett family, in part because Daddy had invested in property during Oklahoma's get-rich-quick oil boom. But no gushers ever spewed black gold from the properties he owned. And then his business failed.

Most of Daddy's customers bought on credit, just signing a sales slip which was then put on a spike with other receipts which he would sort at the end of each day. His customers were his friends; he knew them all, children included, as it was often a child who was sent to the store, sometimes several times a day, to pick up a loaf of bread or a quart of milk.

As the country headed into the Great Depression and the Oklahoma oil boom began to bust, Daddy carried the debts of his customers from month to month as their ability to pay faltered: his generosity exceeded his business acumen. One of my earliest memories is of our packing up our things, leaving Duncan by train, without car or furniture, for Oklahoma City where a relative offered hope for the future. That hope was short lived, however, and the family moved again, this time to Edmond, Oklahoma, where my parents operated a small cafe serving the students who attended the teachers' college there.

As the Depression deepened, my parents could not make ends meet with the diminishing income from the cafe and with our expanding family: Ann was born the day after I turned eight years old. When a cousin offered free rent for a house in Norman, Daddy gratefully accepted.

While Daddy looked for work, Mother skillfully stretched the available food to feed six of us. Still, one day Daddy passed out from hunger walking the railroad tracks from our house to the university where he had gone to look for work.

Our first house in Norman sat on a large lot that backed up to the railroad tracks. Interurban cars ran back and forth from Norman to Oklahoma City, a distance of fifteen or twenty miles, many times a day, and the passenger and freight trains of the Atcheson, Topeka and Santa Fe lines passed frequently. Mary and I watched for the trains and exchanged waves with the engineer and passengers. Hoboes often rode in empty freight cars and that added to the excitement. Many would find their way to our back door asking for food. Even with the little food we had, Mother never turned them away. She served the food to them just as she would to the family, with the hot food hot and the cold food cold. They bragged on her cooking—butter beans with ham hock, cornbread, a glass of buttermilk, and always a sugar cookie or a piece of gingerbread or cake—and no doubt spread the word that ours was a good place for a handout.

Mary and I stayed indoors to play when the days became shorter and colder. It can get really cold in Oklahoma for there's most often a strong wind to accompany sleet, hail, and snow. There was one room in the house we never used: it saved on the heat bill to keep that room closed off and we didn't have furniture to put in it. It was a big room, well lighted with several windows, but it was freezing cold in there. That didn't keep Mary and me from putting on our coats and knitted caps and gloves and making that room our permanent paper doll house. We could set up our paper dolls and leave them undisturbed until we came to play with them another day.

There was no television then, and we were new in the neighborhood, but our paper doll community gave Mary and me plenty to do. Mary was too old to really "play" paper dolls, but she played along with me by making the furniture for the pretend houses. We created elaborate wardrobes for our paper dolls, clothes for every occasion, from diapers to extravagant outfits for being presented at a royal court. We constructed houses and furniture from cardboard, using straight pins to fasten the parts together. (This was before the time of Scotch tape.) We made little bookshelves with shelves pinned in place and we made books to go on the shelves. There were several paper doll families and several houses for them to live in. The best part was that we could leave our "mess"—just close the door when Mother called and take up were we left off the next day.

Mary and I spent many hours bundled in coats, scarves and gloves creating fabulous lives for our little paper friends. The hours from after school to suppertime were ours to live in our imaginations and to build a companionship that would hold us close the rest of our lives.

Thousands of families were, like ours, financially poor during the Great Depression. Short on money, but long on family solidarity and simple pleasures, I know now that I was indeed a rich little poor girl.

ђ

BYE-LO BABY: CHRISTMAS 1927

William Lloyd Lockett

Lloyd was nine years older than I was, and when I was seven, he was a rowdy, flashy, self-centered, girl-crazy teenager. He was quite good-looking with a high forehead (a sure sign of good breeding and intelligence, according to our mother) and a well-shaped head crowned with soft light brown hair. His lips were full but finely delineated, his nose straight and strong, and his eyes were as blue as the Oklahoma skies. That he was a six foot tall, broad-shouldered football player added to his attraction. To top it all, he drove around the little town of Edmond, Oklahoma, in a Ford Tin Lizzie with a rumble seat! His sweet, shy smile belied the devil in him. He was popular. He was wild. He was—for me—unavailable. He was too full of himself to pay much attention to this little sister, but Lloyd made Christmas Day 1927, a wonderful day for me, a day I have remembered all these years.

Although the Great Depression had not yet devastated the country as it was to do in the next several years, hard times had already hit our big family. I was too young to realize how desperately my parents tried to make a good Christmas for us. I looked forward to Christmas and Santa's bounty with all the confidence of a true believer. Gifts under our tree may have been sparse for the older children, but for me, with the special place I then held as baby in the family, Santa came through. There under the tree was a longed-for Bye-Lo baby doll.

The popularity of the Bye-Lo baby doll was similar to that of Cabbage Patch dolls in later years. The unique feature of the Bye-Lo doll was its lifelike newborn face. Its porcelain head was shaped like a brand new baby's, and its face was crinkled like a little one just out of the womb. The Bye-Lo's cloth body was filled with Kapok to make it soft and cuddly.

Tiny porcelain hands protruded from long sleeves with their lace-trimmed ruffled cuffs. Its long white dress was like a christening dress, made of a soft lawn fabric, with tiny tucks in the bodice, and a small round embroidered collar. Little buttons with real button holes at the back neckline made dressing the doll possible but difficult for seven year old fingers to manipulate. It didn't cry or say mama. It

Mary and Dorothy, circa 1927

didn't have real hair. It didn't wet its diapers. But it was the most beautiful doll in the world and my heart was filled with love for it.

I played with my doll all morning except for going out of doors to gather the candy, nuts, and fruits that Santa had spilled from his pack (we had no chimney for him to come down). There was no need to wear a sweater or coat: it was a beautiful blue-sky balmy day—the kind of day that comes to Oklahoma in winter when least expected.

Early in the afternoon, Mother served our traditional Christmas dinner, roast chicken with cornbread stuffing and cream gravy, home-made cranberry sauce, real candied sweet potatoes, mashed potatoes and green peas (to put in the birds' nest of mashed potatoes), spiced peaches, pickled beets, cornbread (always piping hot cornbread, every main meal, every day of the year), and mincemeat and pumpkin pies with whipped cream. For me, it was exactly what Christmas was meant to be.

Later, as the weather was so inviting, Daddy took Mary (ten years old at the time) and me for a walk—so we could work off some high sugar energy and give Mother a break. I wanted to show my doll to the Connor girls who lived down the street, and after much cajoling, Daddy agreed that I could take my Bye-Lo doll with me. I cradled my doll in my arms and, feeling full of the wonders of Christmas, I skipped a little. I saw the crack in the sidewalk. I saw the dry grass between the sidewalk and the street. But I could not stop my fall.

Daddy gently picked me up as Mary stood in disbelief staring at my Bye-Lo baby whose sweet, sweet China head had splintered into a thousand pieces when it hit the curb and fell into the street.

All the family in the house heard the commotion and came to see what had happened. Mother tried to comfort me. Lloyd picked up all the porcelain pieces—

even the tiny slivers, put them on a cardboard and carried them onto the sleeping porch where the sunshine was pouring in through its many windows. I watched as he cut off bits of white adhesive tape (this was long before the advent of super glue) and, with the patience of a school bus driver, Lloyd put my dolly back together again. It took hours to finish the task. After he put on the last bit of tape, he held up the doll for me to examine. Its head was one mass of crisscrossed tape. One look and I knew poor little Bye-Lo baby needed me and I knew I would love it forever. I threw my arms around Lloyd and hugged him tight. He smiled his shy smile and shrugged his shoulders like it was nothing.

My Bye-Lo baby was the most-loved, favorite doll of all my childhood. I wonder now, seventy-eight years later, if Lloyd knew what a wonderful gift he gave me that Christmas. It was more than the repair of the doll: it was his way of showing I mattered to him. Maybe, in the continuum of life, he's sitting there with his angel wings feeling pleased that I remember.

THE BLUE DIARY

Christmas 1928 was Lloyd's last year in high school. Mary was in junior high, I was in fourth grade, and Ann was almost a year old. Dub must have been teaching at the reform school that year, and it was probably Pat's first year to teach because she left Edmond State Teachers College early to start teaching when she was eighteen.

Daddy had landed a job as janitor at the University of Oklahoma on the other side of town a few months after we came to Norman, and we moved to a small house on Tonhawa Street a few blocks from downtown. It was there that we celebrated Christmas in 1928.

As was our custom, we decorated our tree the day before Christmas. Swags of saved sparkling tinsel entwined the tree, as did strands of popcorn and cranberries, and strings of folded paper dolls Mary and I made from colored art construction paper. With Mother's casual supervision, Mary and I laid cotton snow on the top of the branches, thickest toward the trunk and tapering to almost nothing at the branch tips. We put more on the north (back) side of the trunk than the real life warmer south (front) side. If either of us tossed tiny wads of cotton to imitate the snow falling from the sky, Mother tsked-tsked us because we were breaking the rules of how our tree was to be decorated. No shortcuts to get through faster. It was the same with the foil icicles: they were to be applied singly in long silvery strands. Dumping on the Lockett's Christmas tree was not okay. I think this meant we were proud. We cared. And to this day, seventy-six years later, I have strung icicles, one by one, on the trees in my own home. On the rare occasion when I've placed more than a single strand at a time, I've felt a bit guilty—as if I'd not come up to my mother's expectations.

Mary was my playmate, my mentor, and my tormentor. Three years older than I, she took it upon herself to teach me, to help me, to scold me, to spend time with me with stories and secrets, to

Dorothy and Mary, circa 1935

tease me and tickle me under the arms until I would lose my breath. She was deemed so smart she'd already skipped several grades at school. While I knew how giggly and silly Mary could be, to most people she seemed studious, serious and mature for her years.

Was that why she fell through the cracks that Christmas of 1928? How could it happen that there were no gifts for Mary under the tree? How did poor-but-proud parents cope with the great expectations of an American-style Christmas during those depression years? In our family, it was the older children who bought the toys that made Santa real for the smaller ones. Pat, especially, brought the spirit of Christmas with her when she came home from her teaching job with secrets and surprises in the boxes and bags she carried with her. There was a Christmas-y feel in our house with the decoration of the tree, the aroma of mother's baking and candy-making, and Pat's busy, bossy, jolly presence.

On Christmas morning we awakened early to see what Santa had brought. The stockings were filled, and Mother's devil's food cake and milk we'd left for Santa were gone. As always, there was a trail of hard candies on the roof top, on the sidewalk and front porch where they fell from Santa's bag as he scuttled from the rooftop to the front door: we had no chimney.

Santa's bounty of gifts went mostly to little Ann. For me, there was a big doll, presumably to compensate for last year's poor little Bye-Lo baby. I had tripped and my doll's delicate porcelain head was smashed to smithereens when she fell from my arms to the pavement. No doll, not even a big, new one, would ever mean as much to me as my Bye-Lo with its head held together with crisscrossed adhesive tape. My love for Bye-Lo and for Lloyd who repaired her was strong and true. But for Mary; there was no gift under the tree.

Not old enough to play Santa like Dub, Pat and Lloyd, was Mary at eleven too old to be included as a kid? As all the others' gifts were opened, Mary did not show her feelings. She made no mention of it. Nor did the rest of us.

Lloyd silently left the room. I followed him and we made a beeline for downtown. Lloyd knew the drugstore would be open for a while on Christmas morning. If only we could get there in time. Lloyd was hell-bent to get to Pirtle's Drugs before it closed. I struggled to keep up with my brother's fast pace. He may have wished that I hadn't tagged along, but I, too, was determined. While he took long, swift strides befitting a six-foot-tall, eighteen-year-old athlete, I willingly puffed and panted a few feet behind him. He never took my hand to help me keep up, even when I slowed a bit to savor the sweet fragrance of banana oil—it smelled just like the two-for-a-penny banana candies I liked so much—as we passed the automobile repair shop.

We made it. And we found the perfect gift for Mary: The blue leather diary in the glass display case was just right. It had a golden lock and key with the words My Diary engraved in gold on the cover. It came in a pretty box. Lloyd quickly paid for it, and we rushed home to put the diary under the tree and pretend it had been there all the time.

While Lloyd went into the house by the front door, I diverted attention by going in the back door to find out when breakfast would be ready. Soon Lloyd called out, "Hey, look what I found."

We all went into the living room and there was Mary's diary almost hidden in the snow on a low back branch of the tree. So inconspicuously placed, you'd think it really could have been there all the while.

Mary went along with the charade and seemed genuinely pleased with the gift. We all sat down to a wonderful Christmas breakfast of ham and eggs, hot biscuits and cream gravy, strong coffee, and hot chocolate with marshmallows, and went on with our lives.

I've often wondered what Mary wrote in her diary about that particular Christmas day.

Dorothy and Mary, circa 1938

MY SISTER ANN

Eleanor Ann was born at home in Edmond, Oklahoma, to "Bert" and Walter Lockett, parents of Walter Melancthon, Jr., Susan Patty, William Lloyd, Mary Elizabeth, and Dorothy Louise. "Dub" and Pat attended the state teachers' college in Edmond, Lloyd was in high school, and Mary and I were in elementary school. Daddy ran a restaurant that served breakfast and lunch to students at the college. Mother made pies each morning at home, and, after Mary and I were off to school, she carried them down for the lunch crowd. Mother's lemon meringue pies, with their two-inch-high meringues, were a hit, but there wasn't much hope for the restaurant: signs of the Depression were everywhere

Even so, Mother was happy to have a new baby. Ann took after Daddy's side of the family with dark hair and gray eyes. But something was wrong: Mother's milk did not agree with Ann. She kept losing weight at she was given various formulas the doctor tried. Someone—perhaps a friend or neighbor—suggested buttermilk, and that was the magic that turned a very sick child into a healthy baby. Mother's mother stayed with us that summer, and I'm sure she was impressed with Ann's liveliness of spirit.

Ann and Dorothy, circa 1929

Ann was a precocious, feisty little one, so cute she was on the verge of getting spoiled. With her dark straight hair in a Buster Brown bob, with bangs across her forehead, I think she brought Daddy a lot of joy. One winter we were forced to keep hundreds of baby chicks in our house to keep them from freezing. You'll have to ask Ann why one of those chicks, the one she was holding, was missing a wing.

For Christmas, Mother and Mary and I made clothes for the doll that Pat gave Ann. It came in a wardrobe trunk, the doll standing in one-half of the open trunk, the other side filled with drawers and hangers above. But I don't remember if Ann liked the clothes we made. I only remember that Mother, Mary, and I had such a good time working together.

Mary received a pair of flowered pajamas as a present for graduation from high school. Soon they were missing. We looked everywhere we could think of, but no pajamas. Summer turned to fall before they were found stuffed between the mattress and springs of Mary's bed. The culprit: Ann. I know she didn't get a spanking as that wasn't our parents' way, but it was the last of Ann's waywardness. And the last of my tales of Ann's misdeeds.

Ann went to McKinley Elementary School in Norman, and from there to Norman Junior High and High School. She was a good student, was on the honor roll and belonged to a group of girls called "JUG" (Just Us Girls). She went to McFarlin Methodist Church; she could sing; she looked pretty with her straight dark hair that she tried to make curly. I once gave her a gift certificate for a permanent: the operator at the beauty parlor let the mixture stay on too long and her hair was really frizzy. After that she rolled it with hair pins and rollers.

Ann will celebrate her 80th birthday next Saturday.

♄

Dorothy and sister Ann, circa 2004

CHICKENS IN MY DINING ROOM

In the spring of 1930, the Lockett family purchased several hundred just-hatched chicks to raise them to sell as tender young fryers as a supplement to Daddy's paycheck as a janitor at the University of Oklahoma. Side ventures such as this helped desperate families to survive the Great Depression. We brought home from the post office big cardboard boxes with air holes, each filled with one hundred baby chickens.

Although Daddy had prepared the shed in our backyard to put them, the weather turned cold and Daddy proclaimed, "Looks like we'll have to keep them in the house. They'd die out in that shed tonight."

Nobody protested Daddy's judgment. After all, it would only be for a night or two. My sisters and I were delighted in the diversion from routine, and Mother pitched right in to prepare for our new visitors. She found old newspapers to put on the dining room floor. Mary and Daddy brought in the brooder and set it up while the chicks squeezed in their boxes on the kitchen floor loudly cheeped their impatience. Before they could be let out, Daddy had to dream up and make a little fence to keep them corralled in their allotted space. Mother had left a clear passage from the kitchen through a corner of the dining room to the center hall; the rest of the floor was covered with newspaper.

My job was to set up the water containers which were Mason jars filled with water which, when inverted, would let the water seep into a round metal pan with a screw top fitting the jar. This provided maximum space for the chicks to drink without injuring themselves. In their eagerness to drink they would push their way like a stereotypical New Yorker tumbling over each other and crushing their way to the promised land. In this case, the pan of water.

At thirteen, Mary was a responsible adult. I was, at ten, given kid privileges; not much was expected of me. Ann was two, and atypical only that in all the established traits of two-year-oldness, Ann had them twofold. Curious, demanding, cute, feisty, mischievous...a melt-your-heart sweetness could turn in a flash to an unrelenting insistence to "do it myself." What combination of those spirits inside her caused one little chick to lose its wing lying there in her hand? Did she love it too hard? Was the wing so fragilely attached it just fell off when she picked it up...by the wing? Although Ann is known for her kind and gentle nature, some sibling at a family reunion is bound to find a way to bring up Ann's cruelty to baby chicks. It took me years to understand why Mother would say life was best with a two-year-old underfoot.

So what happened, where's the suspense, where's the big problem and the clever solution? Why is this among my memoirs? What happened is the chickens overstayed their welcome.

Day after day, chickens dominated our lives. Chickens escaping through the fence equals chickens in the kitchen, chicken under beds, and chickens into closets. Chickens eating constantly, as they did, equals an overload of chicken shit. Chicken fights. Chickens smothering each other seeking warmth and comfort from their kind. There's the problem. The solution? Finally, the weather changed, the chickens were put outside in the shed with its surrounding grassy fenced yard. The chickens and the Lockett family were back where they belonged.

When it comes to bragging rights, I guess living with chickens in your dining room is about as unusual as a kid needs to talk about. But there's a down side. Even during the Great Depression, there was a stigma attached to chickens in the house. How did my parents handle this with such aplomb?

Mother was brought up in Carlock, Tennessee, where her father was a successful merchant and her mother a pillar of the community. A southern belle who attended a finishing school, Mother probably never imagined a circumstance where she would have chickens in the room where china cupboards and silver chests belonged. After his mother died when Daddy was a boy, he lived at the home of his Uncle Melville, an attorney in Austin, Texas, and before coming to Oklahoma, Daddy attended the university in Austin. For a time, Daddy, too, was a merchant, owner of the Sunshine Mercantile Company in Duncan, Oklahoma. According to the local newspaper, my parents, Walter and "Bert" Lockett were a popular couple in Duncan. They seemed ill-suited to have chickens in the dining room, undeserving of the harsh challenges they faced.

As a child I didn't discern the despair they must have felt. They weren't complainers. Mother's tears could have easily have been for the joy that the chicks were saved from freezing as for the fear of unpredictable pending disasters. There were no social cushions in place—no unemployment benefits, no Social Security, no Medicare or health plans. Only by the grace of the local grocer where credit was given to reliable families like ours was there food on the table for the six of us. And baby brother Jack was only a few months from being born.

This episode in our family's life confirms for me the thread that runs through my memories, that being part of a whole, where there's an acceptance of being together, of doing your part, doing what needs to be done in the comfort zone of a loving family.

Raising baby chicks to supplement Daddy's paycheck as a janitor for the University of Oklahoma was continued when we moved to a little house in the country. We rented the house on Berry Road, a mile west of Norman, because it sat on ten acres of fertile soil. Daddy was optimistic: this could mean a financial turnaround for the family. It meant having an outdoor toilet and bathing in washtubs, but there'd be less cost for food and the rent of $25 a month was a savings over the rent on Tonhawa. There was a good shed for the baby chicks where they would be warm and dry, and Daddy had made a good deal on a milk cow. Enthusiasm ran high as we entered this new adventure.

We had lived on Berry Road for a couple of years when baby brother Hoyl was born. My oldest sister Pat, a grade school teacher in a little town near Tulsa, regularly sent part of her salary to help support the family. My oldest brother Dub sent what he could spare, for no matter how hard Daddy and Mother worked, it seemed we could never catch up. Daddy needed a truss for a double hernia and Mother had a scary encounter with erysipelas: there was no cushion for anything but the bare necessities. There were signs of exhaustion from overwork and worry. It seemed the Depression would never end.

A new batch of several hundred baby chicks, now in a proper home of their own in the shed about a hundred feet from the house, was always cause for excitement for Ann, Jack and Hoyl, and even for me, now in junior high school. One morning, shortly after Daddy had everything going smoothly for the newest chicks, I was awakened by a weird noise, a strange yelping, gasping sound coming from the backyard. Frightened, I ran to a window in the living room and saw my Daddy, flinging our dog around by its tail, flinging and flinging. And the poor dog was yelping on each downswing, the sound getting weaker as Daddy continued his wild flinging. I couldn't cry out. I ran to Mother standing on the back steps, and we stood holding each other and waiting for the torment to end.

The dog had worked its way into the shed, killing over two hundred chicks.

I had never seen my Daddy do a violent thing. I had never been spanked in my life. This was my Daddy who played checkers and dominoes with us, the Daddy we relied on to tell us when to go to the storm cellar, and the Daddy who sat on the porch singing songs with me while we peeled peaches for Mother to can.

Mother did not interfere. She knew how bad things were; she knew this was the act of a man sick with worry about her and their children. This act of a desperate man was understood and forgiven.

♮

SUMMERTIME IN THE COUNTRY

Living in the country was a new experience for the Lockett family. In the spring of 1932, when I was in the sixth grade, we moved from our modest house on Tonhawa Street near downtown Norman to a tiny four-room house on ten acres on Berry Road, a mile west of town. The rent was $25 a month and Daddy wrote in a sometime journal that he kept how high his hopes were that this move would be the turning point—that we could survive the great economic depression that had hit the country and our big family. There were many mouths to feed and his salary as a janitor at the University of Oklahoma in Norman didn't cover our needs.

With a place for a cow, some pigs and chickens, a family vegetable garden, and enough land for grazing and possibly for a cash crop to add to our income, however, Daddy's optimism was infectious. We made the move to Berry Road in time for spring planting.

Mother was pregnant again, her ninth and last pregnancy. She was forty-seven years old and Daddy was fifty-five. In December of that year, Hoyl was born. Hoyl's arrival made six of us kids living in the little bathless, waterless, closetless house on Berry Road. Together with Mother and Daddy, and George, a university student who helped farm the ten acres for his room and board, it was a miracle we didn't step on each other's toes and tempers. Yet my memories of that time of my life are full of sweetness.

On a typical hot summer day, I awakened to the early morning encouragement of the risen sun. The bedroom where I slept was on the east side of the house and was the coolest. It was wall-to-wall beds. Mary and I slept in one double bed with Ann and wiggly Jack in another. Baby Hoyl had a crib by my parent's bed in the living room. By the time I was up and about each morning, Daddy had already prepared and eaten his breakfast, leaving sufficient Cream of Wheat for Mother's morning meal. He left for work early, so Mother usually milked the cow, setting wide bowls of strained milk on the kitchen counter for the cream to rise. Although Mary and I did chores, Mother was not a stern taskmaster and we were not required to get up at a set time. Although we often helped with milking the cow and feeding the chickens and pigs first thing in the morning, it was not demanded of us.

Each weekday morning, usually at churning time, Mrs. Roberts, a neighbor who lived about a quarter-mile to the south of us, came to our house. She and mother would visit while I walked about the same distance north to get the mail for her and for us. Mrs. Roberts was a plain-spoken, friendly woman who admired

Mother's homemaking skills. Mother was fastidious in handling food, especially milk, making sure the straining cloth was tightly secured with clothespins. A straining cloth was needed for two reasons — sometimes cow hairs or other debris could get into the milk pail during milking, and inside, flies were a problem. One morning, Mrs. Roberts expressed her appreciation. "Oh, Mrs. Lockett, you sure take care strainin' your milk. At our place, we don't strain at all. We just hair the butter."

I dreaded going for the mail. I was scared of the crows. The quiet walk to River Road where the mailboxes were located should have been bliss for me as there were always scissor-tail flycatchers, robins, and Baltimore orioles to observe — just when I knew I would grow up to be a famous ornithologist and the scent of the sweet alfalfa that filled the air made each breath a luxury. The Huff family lived at the corner of River and Berry roads and I would sometimes see Dick Huff, who was in my class. We were both too shy to say more than a mumbled greeting, but it was still an event of sorts.

All of these pleasures eluded me when I was told that crows will dive at people and peck out their eyes. There were a whole lot of crows between our house and the mailboxes! I was petrified with the thought of a crow diving at me, but I was ashamed of being afraid: it was hard to protect my eyes while pretending I wasn't a scaredy cat. There was no one to see me. Even so, I contorted my arms and shoulders and head to hide from the crows and any possible observer. It was always an emotional relief to arrive at home with eyes intact.

One day I was well rewarded on my trip to the mailbox. A package from the Crayola Company was addressed to me. My heartbeat quickened, but I waited until I was home to open it. Earlier, I had submitted my coloring of an outline picture of a girl in a bathing suit that appeared in a Crayola contest ad in a magazine. Could I actually have won? The set of sixty-four crayons and a tin watercolor paint box with twenty-four colors that I received was certainly not a first prize, but it was enough to assure me that I would most likely be a famous artist when I grew up.

Ann, Jack and Hoyl were so young they have very little memory of our life in the country. Many of my summertime pleasures came from helping to care for them. They were healthy, active kids that brought to each day unexpected delights. One afternoon we couldn't find Jack to take his nap. We searched in the house and the shed and the outhouse. We were near panic when we discovered him in the pigpen feasting on overripe watermelons with the big, fat porkers.

Noontime was our main meal of the day. During the morning I helped with shelling peas, snapping green beans, peeling peaches for pie, and with other household chores — all tasks that could be done in the relative cool of indoors. I set the table, helped with the little kids, and ate a lot. Mother, from Tennessee, was a wonderful southern cook and we enjoyed biscuits for breakfast, cornbread for lunch, and crumble-in (leftover cornbread broken into cold milk) for supper.

After lunch, I got out of doing dishes by rocking baby brother Hoyl to sleep for his nap. I sat on the front porch nestling him in my arms and fantasizing that some stranger in the night might leave a baby wrapped in swaddling clothes on our door step. I would be the heroine, finding the baby and insisting that we had plenty of room for another little one at our house. There was no doubt that I would become famous for my kind deeds.

Afternoons on those hot Oklahoma summer days were spent warding off the heat. Mother let Mary and me dress as scantily as she thought "decent" (her minimum standard!) until Daddy was due home. These were the days I read stories of Tabitha and other almost grown-up girls who had lots of adventures alien to my simple life. I must have gone to the movies sometimes as Daddy made notations of expenses in his journal, such as: Dodo, movie—10 cents. Mostly I remember learning to sew, trying to be as accomplished as Mary who made cotton short-pants suits for Jack and Hoyl. She made the finest buttonholes, each stitch exactly the same as the last. Afternoon time was also embroidery time: I did red line embroidery on flour sack dishtowels, one for each day of the week. Each towel had a separate design with a bonneted lass performing a typical domestic task. Monday washing, Tuesday ironing. It was important to make the stitches regular and in-line. Mother expected the back side to look as perfect as the top side, and it made no difference that the towels were used, bleached flour sacks. Redoing unacceptable stitching made me a slow but proud embroiderer.

Supper was not always a sit-down meal. Often we ate cold leftovers, crumble-in, or sandwiches. Homemade pimiento cheese was my favorite sandwich. I liked it best with an ice cold Delaware Punch; the soft drink was more of a treat than a regular thing. After supper, Mother would often say, "I'll clean up the kitchen. You go play with your Daddy." Playing with Daddy usually meant dominoes, sometimes checkers, or Rook. There were many evenings, when the heat of the day diminished, that Daddy and I would go out on the ten acres and I would help hoe the weeds. I remember these as easy, quiet times, just being there working together. He liked to tease me. More than once he tricked me into a squeal of fright, especially when we were hoeing the sweet potatoes where the vines covered most of the clear space between the rows. "Watch out, Dodo. There's a rattler!" I never failed to jump and scream, but the rattlesnake was never found. Sometimes he cured me of the hiccups that way.

In the coolness after dark, Mary and I often sat on the porch singing camp songs we had learned at Methodist camp and sharing sister-talk. The flicker of the fireflies sparkling in the night is vivid in my memory as I think of whiling away those happy hours with Mary.

My summers on Berry Road were simple, uncluttered with "getting and spending," surely unsophisticated by today's standards. I marvel that my parents, in those tough times, created in our home an atmosphere of encouragement, vitality, and love. Values I learned then have anchored me these many decades of my life.

The Lockett Family; Walter, Mary, Susan, Dorothy, Dub, Ann, Pat, Jack, Lloyd and Hoyl, circa 1935

THE SUMMER OF LOVE

For Hoyl on his 69th birthday, December 4, 2001

Mrs. Williams taught eighth grade English at Norman (Oklahoma) Junior High School. She was a small dark-haired woman impeccably groomed, probably forty or fifty (how can a kid really tell?), and the kind of dresser who wore a simple black dress with collars and cuffs that could be changed to make it seem like a different outfit. I was in her first period class. Unlike other teachers, she was always at the door greeting her students as they came to class. When the bell rang she closed the door, came into the big high-ceilinged room, and work began. No fooling around in her class, but even so, she was my very favorite teacher. That is, until the morning of December 4th, 1932.

Walter and Susan Lockett

It was on that clear, cold December morning that I was bursting with good news: I wanted to share it first with Mrs. Williams. I bounded up the stairs of the old red sandstone building, took a left toward my English class, and saw her there at the door. A few students were ahead of me. When it was my turn, I blurted out, "Guess what, Mrs. Williams! I have a new baby brother! He was born last night and his name is John Hoyl and he weighs..."

Something in her look stopped me short. In a bored, condescending tone, she asked, "So? How many does that make?" Humiliation engulfed me as the kids standing next in line sniggered.

How dare she be so arrogant! The fact is Hoyl was the eighth child in our family—and that's not counting Baby Catherine, who died ten years before when she was only a few weeks old. No matter. And no matter that my parents were old enough to be Hoyl's grandparents. (Mother was forty-seven and Daddy was fifty-five.) What if we were poor and lived in a tiny house in the country? Or that my Daddy was a janitor at the university? Or that I wore hand-me-down, made-over clothes that smelled like coal smoke from the pot-bellied stove that kept us warm? No matter what Mrs. Williams thought or said, John Hoyl Lockett was a wanted child. There was plenty of room in our little house and our big hearts to welcome him into our family.

With that snide remark, Mrs. Williams told me more about herself than pleased me. It was one of life's bitter lessons to improve my skill in judging character. She crashed with such force off that pedestal where I had so lovingly put her that the pieces of her Most Favorite Teacher status could not be put back together again. I endured first period English until summer vacation set me free.

I was probably the most unsophisticated thirteen-year-old in Oklahoma that summer of 1933; happy to be barefoot in the country—oblivious to the strivings of my peers in town where the influence of the university's tight fraternity/sorority caste system dictated the social behavior of teens in junior high and high school. The sweet smell of the alfalfa fields that bordered the ten acres where we lived on Berry Road a mile west of Norman, and the captivating sight of the scissor-tailed flycatchers balancing on the high utility wires with their foot-long split tails holding them steady as each puff of a breeze or a sway of the wire threatened their status quo—those were everyday delights for me. Living in the country suited me just fine.

Even with the two oldest away from home, our family packed that tiny house. In addition to Mother and Daddy (who slept in the living room), there was little Hoyl in a crib beside them; sister Mary, three years older than I; feisty four-year-old Ann; and two-year-old Jack, curly-haired and cuddly; and I had the front bedroom; and my six-foot athlete brother, Lloyd, a summertime oil-rigger and a student at the university during the school year, shared the other bedroom with George, a college student who helped Daddy farm the ten acres for his room and board.

As short of money as we were and as hard as she worked, Mother liked her life. Some people whistle while they work: Mother touched her teeth together and softly hissed a little tune as she went about her chores. Mary and I helped. Mother was persnickety about our doing every job well, but she was a gentle task-master.

There was always work to do. Lots of beds to make, slop jars to empty, water to bring from the well, eggs to gather, dishes to wash, peaches to peel, beans to snap and peas to shell, and then, more dishes to wash. Always, always, little kids to care for, to clean and diaper and dress and entertain. Mornings were the busiest part of the day as our main meal was served at midday.

Main meal in our house meant meat and potatoes and cream gravy, fresh peas or beans, sliced tomatoes, pickled beets, cucumbers, bell pepper, cold milk or buttermilk, and fresh-baked hot, crispy cornbread every day served with home-churned butter and homemade preserves or jelly. For dessert, Mother would bake fresh peach cobbler drenched with rich, fresh cream—or a tart lemon pie with a perfect two-inch meringue. Invariably on Sundays we finished our meal with Mother's special red devil's food cake with a thick fudge frosting which she cooked in a big iron skillet. Mary and I vied to beat the frosting as the privilege of scraping the fudge-coated skillet went to the beater.

We were poor, but you can see that we ate well. Mother who was brought up in Tennessee was an inspired southern cook. White leghorn chickens laid plenty of eggs and provided the meat for Mother's scrumptious fried chicken (guaranteed fresh and tender as Mother would wring their necks and pluck the feathers from the one-pound fryers just before she fried them). Mother milked the cow, and Daddy occasionally butchered one of our hogs. Ten acres of garden gave us food throughout the year. Mother was a meticulous canner, placing peach halves with only the round side up in the jars. The Kentucky Wonder green beans stood in their Mason jars precisely side by side like tin soldiers at attention. Mother took pride in her handiwork. By the end of summer, more than five hundred quarts of canned vegetables and fruit lined the shelves in the cellar. There was still room for beets, Idaho potatoes, sweet potatoes and peanuts—an abundance to feed us through the winter.

With everything that was served being processed from the farm to the family table, there were tons of dishes to wash and dry, especially after our noontime meal. It was long before the day of detergents and automatic dishwashers. Doing the dishes then was a time-consuming, tedious task, especially as we had to bring in the water from the well, and discard the dishwater later in the pigs' trough. Scrubbing the pots and pans meant just that, scrubbing. Fels-Naptha soap was the best available, but the greasy soap scum offended my tender teenage sensibilities. I was a reluctant dishwasher, and somehow weaseled my way out of doing the dishes and into my summer of love. So it became my daily task, just after the midday meal, to sit on the front porch and rock baby Hoyl to sleep for his afternoon nap.

The house we lived in was a little square portioned into four rooms of equal size, except for the front bedroom. Its size was diminished by the space needed to make a small front porch. By Hoyl-rocking time, the porch was the coolest spot on the whole ten acres. Two big mulberry trees in the front yard gave an added sense of coolness. In my loose, sleeveless, cotton house dress, with only panties underneath, I was dressed as lightly as social custom and Mother would allow; Hoyl was dressed in soft birds' eye cotton diapers. Cool and comfortable, we rocked and rocked. Hoyl nestled in my arms as I softly sang songs I'd learned at Methodist summer camp:

> **Come, let us be joyful while life is bright and gay.**
> **Gather ye roses ere they wither away.**
> **We're always making our lives so blue.**
> **We look for thorns and we find them, too,**
> **And leave the roses quite unseen**
> **That grow to cheer our way!**

It didn't seem to matter to Hoyl that I couldn't carry a tune. He accepted me as surrogate mother for that special time we shared each day. Long after he was asleep in my arms, we rocked...and as I watched a pair of brilliant Baltimore orioles building their hanging basket nest in the nearest mulberry tree, I daydreamed. Nascent maternal instincts stirred in my soul.

Now when Hoyl and I get together we catch up on how we're doing, talk about our families and the relatives, argue politics and feel grateful for our big, close family—and I hold back the tears as I remember the sweetness of those summer days on Berry Road. There will always be a tender place in my heart for my baby brother Hoyl...a bonding that came from that summer of love back in 1933.

♄

Dorothy and Hoyl, circa 2004

PAT'S WEDDING

November 14, 2002

Dear Pat,

HAPPY 93RD BIRTHDAY! With luck and next day air postage this story will arrive on your 93rd birthday. I have reworked this story so many times and I am still far from satisfied with it. However, the time has come to put it behind me and let it be. It was my intention to do it with love and joy and stuff. It may now read like a committee wrote it. Happy Birthday, anyhow. Will be talking with you later today.

Lots of love,

PS: One thing I know for sure: I will never again tell anybody I am going to write a story for or about them. Whatever I do will be a surprise to them and me.

For several years during the Great Depression my family lived on Berry Road, a mile west of Norman, Oklahoma. Like a postage stamp on a manila envelope, the little house we lived in was stuck on the northeast corner of a ten acre rectangle of flat, fertile land. It wasn't much of a house—four rooms, no running water, no bathroom, no closets—but for the big Lockett family, at $25 a month in rent, it was a godsend that helped us survive those desperate years with family intact.

As I look back now, almost seventy years later, life on Berry Road was good. One of my fondest memories is

Susan Patty Lockett and Howard Markley

of the day my sister Pat married Howard in the front room of that little house.

Pat taught fourth grade in Shidler, a desolate, godforsaken oil town north of Tulsa. It was pure luck that Howard, a chemical engineer, came there to work for Phillips Petroleum Company. A blind date brought them together. Pat admired Howard's fine mind, his goodness, and his keen sense of humor behind a studious, quiet manner. Howard marveled at Pat's gaiety, her quick wit and ready laughter, abounding energy, and generous spirit. She accepted his slightly crossed eyes and he her tendency to plumpness. Love prevailed!

It was 1934. She and Howard planned to be married when school was out in June. Pat wanted our brother, Dub, to officiate at their marriage. Dub had recently been ordained a Methodist minister and this would be his first wedding. He and his wife, Helen (who was Pat's good friend from high school days) lived in Virginia and would come to Oklahoma for the wedding in June.

Those plans changed with the unexpected death of Helen's father. She and Dub came to Oklahoma City in time for the funeral on April 24, 1934. Making the trip again for Pat's wedding in June was financially impossible. Saturday, April 24, became the date for the wedding as well.

Pat borrowed her roommate's car (but didn't invite her to the wedding as our house was so small). She and Howard drove to Oklahoma City, attended the funeral, were thankful the court house in Norman opened until noon on Saturday so they could get a license, and arrived on Berry Road to find a waiting, welcoming family. The house was as sparkling as could be. Mother and Daddy's bed and Hoyl's crib had been taken from the front room. The big black coal stove with the coal bucket and poker were not in use on that beautiful day. Wonderful aromas wafted from the kitchen.

With Pat and Howard, Mother and Daddy, Lloyd, Mary and me—and the three little ones—the house seemed full already. I was fourteen. Mary and Lloyd were in college. Six-year-old Ann looked cute and crisp with her Buster Brown haircut. Jack, who would be four in July, and Hoyl, not quite a year and a half, were underfoot. There were more for the wedding: Howard's family—his mother, brother Ted and his wife Ruth, and Ethelyn, Howard's sister. And, of course, Dub and Helen. The wedding wouldn't happen without Dub. When Dub drove up, everyone was surprised that he had brought Helen's mother and sister and a former neighbor, Mrs. Phillips. By that time the walls were bulging. The big oak dining table Lloyd made would seat a crowd, but I have no idea where enough chairs were found for everyone to sit.

After the homemade ice cream and devil's food cake which completed the delicious and bountiful midday meal, Lloyd motioned for me to come outside with him. To my delight he included me in the secret task of decorating the bridal couple's getaway car.

For the ceremony we gathered again in the front room. The wicker settee and all available chairs were placed in rows with Mother's chair near the opening to the kitchen, and with space left near the side wall for Pat and Howard to stand facing Dub. Pat looked pretty in a simple dark blue dress. Howard wore a brown herringbone suit. Except for Pat's corsage and Howard's sole carnation, there were no other fresh flowers. At the sound of Dub's clear, rich voice tears started to flow. Mother and I were especially good at that.

After a while, little Hoyl, who was sitting on Mother's lap became restless, squiggled down to the floor and clanged the poker against the coal bucket. He was not happy when Mother restrained him. She put him back on her lap, reached through the doorway to the kitchen, grabbed a piece of the remaining devil's food cake, stuffed it in Hoyl's mouth, stopped his crying—all the while, with tears flowing, she kept her eyes on center stage.

At one point Dub admonished the bridal couple to attend to the duties imposed by the marriage vows. At least he started to by saying "I charge you..." Before he could continue, Lloyd called out from the back row. "Five dollars." Stern glances shot at Lloyd, a few clucks and tsks could be lip read, but it did enliven the service.

(Several years earlier, Dub and Pat shared an apartment when they both taught in Shidler. They knew each other's habits pretty well. When Dub learned of Pat and Howard's intent to marry, he wrote a letter to Howard. To congratulate him? No, to give him a first-hand account of all of Pat's faults!)

The bride and groom kissed. The wedding was over. The newlyweds drove away down unpaved Berry Road with tin cans banging and crepe paper streamers flying. Just Married was printed in large letters on the back window for all the world to see.

These are some of the things I remember from that long-ago wedding. But the facts don't add up to the feelings I have. To me, that was the loveliest wedding (except my own) I have ever attended. Was Pat so naive that she didn't know about satin dresses with trains, tuxedos with bow ties, and flower girls and the wedding march? Why else would she be married in that tacky little house with Mother wearing her ill-fitting dentures, and guests having to use the outhouse? "That's the only way Mother and Daddy could be there," she told me when I asked her recently. Perhaps that is why I treasure the memories of Pat's and Howard's wedding. It made clear to me the essence of love of family—not just for good times in good times, but for anytime and always.

♭

GINGERSNAPS

The pecking order at the high school in Norman, Oklahoma, in the 1930s mimicked the divisive fraternity/sorority culture that dominated social life at the University of Oklahoma just a few miles away. The elite at Norman High were the members of the exclusive San Souci social sorority. Next in the high school social order came the Gingersnaps, a pep club sponsored by the school. Mrs. Roberts, a middle-aged haughty English teacher, was the club's "mother."

Gingersnaps held closed door meetings in her classroom after school. The pep club followed the sorority practice of pinning pledges. It was a badge of social status to wear the orange and black pledge ribbons.

I never aspired to be pinned by San Souci, but I did expect to be a Gingersnap. I assumed I would be pledged when I entered ninth grade in 1934. My sister Mary who had graduated in the spring had been a Gingersnap all throughout high school and her Gingersnap uniform was waiting for me. On the day the pledge ribbons were handed out, there was none for me. Disappointed, angry, shamed—I forced back the tears as I ran to catch the bus.

The bus took me to the edge of town. From there, it was a mile's walk through alfalfa fields to my house in the country. I thought the quiet walking and the gentle fragrance of the alfalfa would calm me. Instead, I could not control the thoughts of rejection that swelled my sense of desperation.

As I opened our front door, the floodgate of my tears burst. There was my mother, enfolding me in her arms. Not asking what happened, not pressuring me to stop crying, we sat on the old rattan sofa with the sun coming in the west window, she comforted me. Between gut-wrenching sobs, I told her I had been blackballed by the Gingersnaps. I can't remember a word my Mother said. All I remember is that I felt her love

I dreaded going to school the next day. But I knew I could find the courage to face being ignored. No sooner had I arrived at my first class than the Pledged Gingersnaps rushed into the room. "Oh, Dorothy, there was a mix-up yesterday. I tried to catch you as you were running to the bus. Here's your pledge ribbon. Let me pin it on you." I was in!

We wore our Gingersnap uniforms to school on the days there was a football game. I entered into the spirit of the Gingersnaps, yelling myself hoarse in support of the Norman High Tigers, but there was something about being a Gingersnap that didn't agree with me.

I didn't like those secret meetings in Mrs. Roberts's classroom. The way they chose new members grated on my sense of fair play. There was a meanness to it. Any girl nominated to be a new member was at the mercy of the prevailing clique who gleefully savaged the nominee's reputation. The indictments of the nominee were unkind, insensitive, and snotty, attacking her appearance, behavior, friends, and family. Mrs. Roberts went along with it; didn't bother her. Just one NO vote meant the girl was blackballed and the next day everyone at school knew it.

I resigned from the Gingersnaps, but I am grateful to them. I gained knowledge about life and love—knowledge that has helped me set my priorities for seventy years. And wasn't it lucky that I had Mary's hand-me-down uniform? Buying a new one for such a short tenure as an "in" girl would have been a hardship hard for our struggling family in those Great Depression years. Best of all, I realized the wonder of the safety unacknowledged those first fourteen years of my life...the sheer joy of knowing I was loved and free to be me.

♄

MISS MARJORIE STAFFORD

A Thanksgiving exercise for me on this, my eighty-second year, was to think back to people, not family members, who have been especially kind to me or influential in my life. Marjorie Stafford, my boss at the University of Oklahoma Library came instantly to mind.

It was already hot at 8 o'clock in the morning that end-of-summer day in 1938 as I walked the couple of blocks from my family's home at 930 Elm Street in Norman, Oklahoma, to my part-time secretarial job at the Extension Division on the University of Oklahoma campus. My mind felt as sticky and irritable as the weather. In just a few weeks fall semester classes would start and I didn't yet have a suitable job. I could keep the one I had but it was an NYA job and paid 25 cents an hour. (NYA are the initials for National Youth Authority, a work program initiated by President Franklin D. Roosevelt's New Deal to bring the country out of the great depression.) I lived at home and tuition was free for Oklahoma students, so I could manage on the $5 a week I earned, but my ambition was a regular part-time job on the university's administrative staff. Most of those jobs—so those of us who didn't have them thought—went to students who had some "pull." With a university-paid job I would earn 30 cents an hour and could have a job year round.

Although I had submitted resumes at the Administration Office and had applied at the library several times, I had not had any response.

It was not only the money at the Extension Division: the man I worked for was the Director, and from my eighteen-year-old point of view he was a forty-year-old oaf whose intellectual and emotional development had been stunted by four years in a campus fraternity. Sure enough that very morning, he called me in to take dictation. I said to myself, "I bet it's another personal letter." He was sitting with his feet on the desk, master of all he surveyed-- which included gold and silver plated trophies for fraternity athletic events twenty years before. He could hardly keep from patting himself on the back for his wit and charm as he dictated a letter to an old buddy recalling some of their bad boy antics in their fraternity.

That pushed me to immediate action. Although it was noon when I left for lunch, I decided to stop at the Library one more time. I walked across campus to the Library, turned right and entered the office of the librarian, Mr. Rader. His secretary was at lunch, but he saw me. asked if he could help, and invited me to sit down. Our meeting was short, but long enough for me to do two things I did not plan nor approve: one, I invoked the name of his star graduate, Ethelyn Markley, who was well on her way to becoming head of the library sciences department at the University of California, Berkeley. Ethelyn was my sister Pat's sister-in-law. I felt sure she would send a letter on my behalf but I hadn't checked with her before I blurted out her name as a reference. The other stupid thing was that I cried. It was a two or three Kleenex cry. In fact I sobbed. I couldn't stop. Totally humiliated, I left his office lecturing myself and sniffling all the way home.

I had no sooner walked in the door at 930 Elm when the phone rang. It was Mr. Rader's secretary asking if I could come for an interview with Miss Stafford, head of the Order Department, in thirty minutes. My tears of self pity dried right then. I dashed upstairs, changed to a nicer blouse, freshened my make-up and dashed out of the house.

Entering the library, I walked down the long, ornate hall to the Order Department. Miss Stafford was sitting at her desk facing the doorway. She greeted me, showed me where to sit, asked me a few questions and told me a little about the job. She seemed very efficient, a quiet, restrained woman: she might have been imposing but for her small size. I sensed her work was her life. She asked me to file some catalog cards, leaving them on end so she could check my filing skills. Smiling, she said they needed help and that I would be starting the very next day.

♄

TWO YOUNG MEN

"Would you like a cup of coffee?" The words had scarcely left my lips when I realized I was in trouble.

Tom Boyd was sitting at our dining table. Text books and notebooks cluttered the table top. Without premeditation, Tom and I were studying together. A chance meeting at the library, and here he was at my very own house. I can't remember what class it was we had together—I can't even remember his being in a class with me in college—but here he was and I was in a bit of a dither about it.

Tom and I had been classmates for years. We graduated—class of 1937—from Norman High School and went on then to the other side of Norman to attend the University of Oklahoma. He was studying engineering and I was a home economics major. We weren't really friends. I probably had a crush on him but it's hard to remember as I had so many crushes back then.

A superstar in high school, Tom was a top student, popular athlete, and always was elected president of his class. He deserved it all. Tom was a born true leader, in appearance and in character. He stood tall: he was tall and his proud posture emphasized his height and his comfortable self-image. As the son of a medical doctor who served as administrator of the large state-run mental institution in Norman and whose mother was known for her leadership in charitable and social activities, Tom lived a privileged life in our community of about ten thousand townspeople. He did not flaunt his good fortune. Tom was a genuinely good, solid person even through the usually turbulent teens when so many of us are insecure, searching desperately for our unique identity.

While studying that night with Tom, my mind wandered back to another chance—and mortifying—meeting with him a few years earlier.

One of my summertime chores when we lived in the country in the 1930s was to walk our milk cow down to the gully by the main road to the river where she could graze on the little bit of greenery there. The pasture we had on our rented ten acres was dried up with the blazing Oklahoma sun but there always seemed to be a bit of green grass in the gully where the soil was somewhat protected from the heat. I didn't object to this task, even though it was hot outside. I took a book along to read while the cow grazed, but most often I counted petals as I pulled them off black-eyed Susans and daydreamed. I wore just any old thing. There'd be nobody around to notice me, so I dressed for comfort in an old, loose fitting, sleeveless, homemade cotton house dress. (This was before the days when girls wore blue jeans or shorts.) My shoes were old and sloppy to be as cool as possible and still protect my feet from the hot dusty road. (Flip-flops were yet to come.) One day, having staked out the cow, I sat reading and was startled to hear "Hi, Dorothy, how are ya?" I looked up to see this handsome knight on a fine bay stallion who, when the mistiness before my eyes blended into reality, I recognized as Tom Boyd, dressed in jodhpurs and riding boots and looking entirely like an aristocrat. Any greeting to him, or any continuing conversation, completely escapes my memory. If there were companions with him I never noticed. All I wanted was to be out of there, preferably back in my mother's womb. How could it happen that I was wearing that old rotten hanging house dress instead of a tight fitting cashmere sweater (I didn't own one) when Tom Boyd saw me sitting in a gully with an old stupid cow?

Why did I ever offer him a cup of coffee? How stupid could I be? I didn't know how to make coffee. I didn't drink coffee. All I knew about coffee was that wonderful fragrance that wafted up the stairs each morning. as I rushed getting ready for class. As I dashed out the door, I drank the hot cocoa that mother left for me on the newel post. Yet somehow, I put grounds into the coffee pot and quietly suffered as the percolator made its happy burping sounds. When the perking stopped, I poured a rich black gruel into Tom's cup. As I handed it to him I couldn't help but notice that the cup was fatally cracked.

Another fine young man that I knew in my youth was Bill Lyda. In 1939-1940 he frequently walked me home from my night job at the library at the University of Oklahoma in Norman. He, too, was a student at the university. I think he was a year or two ahead of me. Although we shared many pleasant hours together, full of talk and laughter, I can't really remember, after these sixty-plus years that have passed, many particular facts of his life—where he came from, why he chose to come to OU, his family make-up and circumstances, his heritage, religion, or politics.

I remember that Bill, like most students then, struggled to make ends meet to go to college. He never called me for a date to go to the movies or to dinner. Our dates, if they could be called that, amounted to his coming to the Periodical Room where I worked, studying when I was busy and coming to the desk to visit when I was free, then walking me home when the library closed. We were comfortable with that: neither of us looking to the other for romance.

Always sparkling clean and well groomed, Bill was not a classy dresser. He was nice looking but not handsome. A good student, he was not outstanding. Straightforward, honest, he was remarkably unspectacular—except for his magnificent body. Bill's body was that of a classic athlete. From the angular cut of his nose to his flamboyant leg muscles, his physique evoked visions of strength and grace.

He was a star on the OU track team and was justifiably proud of his winnings and his medals. At OU football was king: students and townspeople took very little notice of other sports or their stars. That never seemed to bother Bill. He felt confident and pleased with himself. His was a long, sure stride that kept me double-stepping to keep up with him as we walked under the solid canopy of elm tree branches that led to 930 Elm Street, the home of my parents and three younger siblings where I lived.

For a couple of months in the spring of 1940 I lived at the home economics practice house, a requirement for all home economics majors. The house was also on Elm Street, two or three blocks from where I lived at 930 Elm. Professor Helen Hamill (whom we irreverently called Horseface Hamill—for no reason that I remember except that we were often silly girls) was the director of the practice house. Although I enjoyed the dorm life there, I missed the freedom of living at home where I had no curfews, no locked doors.

That's where I was living one gentle, moonlit night when Bill, walking me home, unexpectedly suggested we go to the Kampus Korner to get a Coke. That suited me fine. Enjoying springtime and youth, we loitered the half mile back to the Korner, lingered over our cokes served in Coca-Cola signature glasses overloaded with cracked ice just the way I liked, when suddenly I remembered the curfew. We were out of there and on our way. Bill, by himself, could have made it in a breeze, but that was hardly the point. I was puffing and panting and plagued with guilt for missing curfew. I was not lucky: The doors were locked. My roommate, sound asleep, didn't respond to our furtive pleas for help.

"No need to worry," I said. "I'll just go home. Mother never locks the door." Mother did that night. Knocking on the door was out of the question. She would not have liked the idea of my being out past curfew.

"Let's try Inez." I suggested. My friend Inez, recently graduated, lived in a little bungalow on the other side of the campus. Was it empathy for my predicament, the lateness of the hour, or the moonlight? As we walked back across campus, Bill's tenderness surprised and pleased me.

All lights were off at Inez's house. She did not respond to our knock on her front door. Bill and I walked to the back of the house, scratched on the screen of her open window, and whispered her name. Without alarm, as if she frequently had nighttime callers, she sat up in bed and sleepily asked "Who is it?" Hearing my name, she immediately became a gracious hostess, welcoming me as if I were an invited guest. Bill walked me to the front door. We parted with a kiss.

The earth-rattling ring of Inez's alarm clock awakened me in time to arrive at the practice house safely. I felt conspicuous walking across campus in its early morning inactivity. My roommate spied me and slipped me in through the kitchen door. Professor Hamill never knew.

As for Bill and me, he graduated and left Norman when the term was over. I transferred to the University of Nebraska in the fall.

Tom Boyd and Bill Lyda were killed in World War II.

PART TWO: MY LATER EARLY YEARS

HEY ROMEO

The few blocks to the south and east of East Warren and Gladwin were the center of my life for the first part of the year I lived in Detroit in 1948. On the west side of East Warren was the new Motor City Co-op, where I worked. Across the street, on the northeast corner, was the huge, sprawling, noisy, ugly Briggs Auto Parts factory. Henry and Mary's cafe was on the southeast corner.

New Motor City Co-op, 11555 E. Warren, Detroit, MI, circa 1948

Twenty-eight, single, and idealistic, I had come to Detroit when offered the job as education secretary at the co-op. Intensely involved in my work, I found the right place to live only a block away. A nondescript place with tan colored fake-brick exterior, the house faced the Briggs factory. Archie Bunker would have felt at home there. A half dozen steps led to a front porch barely large enough to hold a wooden swing. To get to my room, I walked through the small living room, past the bathroom, through the kitchen and up the narrow stairs to the attic. Remodeled to bring in extra income, the attic area had very little standing space. The ceiling sloped sharply on both sides but if I toed the straight and narrow I could walk upright down the center of the room. Beyond a small sitting area, a bed and dresser filled the space. A dormer window looked out over the noisy delivery dock at the Briggs plant.

In late May or early June of 1948. I met my soulmate in front of the soups at the new co-op market on East Warren Avenue in Detroit. It wasn't that our shopping carts collided and, in disentangling them, our fingers touched, our eyes met and zing! we were in love.

It was more like this:

"Hi. I overheard your conversation just now. You did a fine job explaining the co-op to those two women: you know a lot about co-ops! We could sure use you on our education committee. It meets here Monday night. Oh, excuse me. I'm Dorothy Lockett. I work here. I came from Rochdale Co-op in D.C. a couple weeks ago to be education secretary."

"Hi, Dorothy. I heard you were here—and doing a great job. I'm Bob Hansen. I've been working at the little Pontiac co-op. They loaned me to come over here to help out for the next few months, until we get started on the new Flint co-op. I'll be working nights mostly. But yeah, I'd like to help out on the education committee. What time does the meeting start?"

"Seven-thirty."

"I'll be there."

"Thanks, Bob. We'll be so glad to have you."

While this chatter was going on, I was thinking, Wow, he's really a nice guy. Easy smile. Blue eyes, brown hair—just like mine. And tall, very tall. Maybe he looks so tall because he holds his head up high: self-assured, confident. No bulging muscles like a weight lifter, but he looks strong. Look at the size of those hands. Looks smart, too. Wholesome and clean—like an overgrown Boy Scout. Maybe not that goody-goody, but there is absolutely nothing sophisticated about him. You know, I even think he smells good: none of that icky Old Spice perfume smell I can't stand. We'll see what he's like on the committee. Low-key as it was, that was the auspicious beginning of our fine romance, a love affair that lasted fifty years.

Bob Hansen was twenty-eight, single, and idealistic too. He had come to Detroit to work for the co-op. He stayed in a rooming house a short walking distance from the co-op. I shared space in a modest home a block east on Gladwin. Before long it became a habit for us and for some of our co-workers to meet at Henry and Mary's for breakfast.

Henry and Mary's catered to the workers at Briggs and other factories nearby. Briggs workers wore overalls

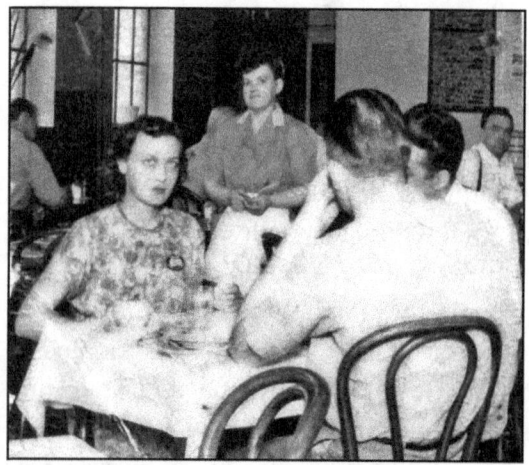

Dorothy and Bob at Henry and Mary's, circa 1948

and hard hats; they were the backbone of Henry and Mary's business. In we came, employees at the new co-op whose "citified" dress set us apart. That distinction, however, was soon blurred by the fact that Briggs workers became members of the co-op, some serving on committees and on the board of directors.

Henry and Mary met the challenge with ease, serving plates full of tender flapjacks, super-size bowls of cereal, and big cups of hot coffee to tables covered with white cloths and with centerpieces of fresh flowers.

At work and at Henry and Mary's, as Bob and I felt the sweet beginnings of romance, we learned to know each other's ways. Bob's happy disposition showed itself early in the morning. He arrived at breakfast fresh and glad for a new day, and often with a silly pun rolling off his tongue—so early in the morning! I, on the other hand, with an inner clock guaranteeing that I would be late no matter what the appointed time, struggled to get to Henry and Mary's in time for an orange juice, coffee, and cigarette before work.

A man of action, Bob saw to it that I had time to eat a decent meal. Every morning, he walked from his rooming house to my home, and, so as not to disturb my landlady, he stood on the sidewalk outside my house, picked up a few pebbles and threw them gently at my dormer window until I woke up. Getting up wasn't my favorite thing and I often awakened groggy and grouchy. I would acknowledge his thoughtfulness by dragging myself to the dormer and waving some sort of feeble greeting. Sometimes it was very difficult to awaken me, so more tosses, more pebbles. One morning when I did not respond after repeated attempts to awaken me had failed, Bob heard a booming voice through the loudspeaker on the loading dock down at Briggs. "Hey, Romeo, use a brick!"

With his waiting so patiently for me, and with my increasing desire to be with him, I dressed quickly and we held hands as we walked down the block together.

Bob and I were married a couple of months later, on November 5, six months after we met. For fifty fine years, he was always the first one up in the morning. He awakened me with a cup of hot coffee, a glad-for-a-new-day attitude, and often with a silly, sickly pun. Whenever he was asked what he attributed to our success, he would feign a macho attitude and say, "Well, I just beat her up every morning." But he never used a brick!

OH, HAPPY, HAPPY WEDDING DAY

For Bob and me it was six months from meeting to marriage. We might as well have worn matching "Made for Each Other" tee-shirts on that day we met at the food co-op in Detroit. Our relationship went from attraction to love as naturally as if our paths had been waiting to cross. We were so moony my landlady compared us to a couple of sick cows in a snowstorm. When, in his sometimes quaint, old-fashioned way, Bob—on bended knee—asked, "Will you marry me?" my answer was quick and positive: "I will. I will. I will." We shared tender tears of joy. We then took a bus out East Warren to Sid's Place where we toasted our good fortune and our future with salubrious old-fashioneds.

Dorothy and Bob's wedding day, 11-5-1948

We set the date for Friday, November 5, 1948. That gave us a few weeks to get rings, an apartment, and a preacher. A wedding bash was not our style. With my parents in Oklahoma and siblings scattered all over; with Bob's parents in New Jersey, and, as newcomers to Detroit, we knew only our co-workers at Motor City Co-op, it was easy for us to plan a simple marriage ceremony.

Both Bob and I had been churchgoers when we were young, but we were now twenty-eight and hadn't been to church in years. It was our boss, Jack McLanahan (He still takes credit for bringing Bob and me together—Bob from New England co-ops and me from Washington, D.C.'s Rochdale Co-op) who arranged for the preacher and for us to be married in the choir stall at Detroit's First Methodist Church. Except for our two witnesses, Israella "Rae" Austin and Hank Warren, no guests were invited. Having a reception never occurred to us.

We were to be married at nine o'clock in the morning. With only Friday—our wedding day—off from work, we planned to go directly from the church across the bridge to Windsor, Ontario, Canada for a weekend honeymoon. It was a cold day in Detroit the day before the wedding. We were all set. Bob was going to wear his one and only suit and I would wear my favorite dress, a dark blue silk shantung with a small, rounded double collar, slanted neck closing, fitted waist and circular skirt. Bob had made arrangements for flowers and photographs, and I was to leave work early to get my hair and nails done. Hank had loaned us his car for the weekend. It was gassed up and ready to go.

Then the telegram came: **ARRIVING DETROIT AIRPORT – 10:30 P.M. TONIGHT – TWA FLT 482 – MOM AND POP.**

It never occurred to us that Bob's parents would attend our wedding. We had not issued invitations to either of our parents or his brother or all my brothers and sisters. It wasn't that kind of wedding. We were just going to stand there before a preacher, say our vows, and leave. I didn't know his parents. I had never met them. I didn't know if they'd like me. Besides, I had never known any Norwegians before. Now we had to go to the airport and meet them and entertain them and I didn't even know them. Our plans went awry, and my nerves went with them.

By the time we arrived at the airport, we had heard on the radio that planes leaving LaGuardia were delayed because of a severe storm. TWA Flight 482 was among those. We waited. And waited. Past midnight. No Mom and Pop. All planes cancelled. Abandoning our plan for a Windsor weekend, Bob and I drove back to Detroit. About two in the morning we stopped by the co-op, checked out a supply of groceries for the weekend, delivered them to our yet-to-be-lived-in apartment, then went to our rooming houses. For the next few hours, I lay in my bed, exhausted, too wound up to sleep, waiting for the alarm to ring.

It was cold and raining that 5th of November morning in Detroit. Bob had the flowers with him when he came to pick me up. When I saw the size of the orchid corsage Bob pinned on me, I said "It's really lovely, but you shouldn't have spent so much money." "I didn't." he said. "The florist gave it to me. She said I looked so much in love she didn't have the heart to charge me for it!"

Mom and Pop were sitting in the sanctuary when we arrived at the church. They had come by train and looked as tired as we felt. Frank and Rae and the preacher were there, as were a half dozen uninvited coworkers sitting in the choir loft. The ceremony began, using the standard text but modified to exclude any reference to "obey" in the vows. Bob and I cried profusely all the while, prompting the minister to remark on our great love for each other. True, but he didn't know how sleep deprived we were.

Rae and Hank were to meet us for lunch at The Gables. The Gables was a gracious country inn outside Detroit where Bob and I lingered over dinner most every payday during our courtship. We were well known to the staff there, some, including Mrs. Townsend, the owner, who surely had observed our blossoming romance.

With Mom and Pop in tow, we showed them where we worked and then took them to our apartment. It was time for me to get acquainted with my new in-laws. Easy enough with Pop, outgoing, self-assured, big and blustery. Not as tall as Bob, who was over 6' 3". Pop was squarer—but strong like Bob. He looked like the carpenter/contractor he was. With Mom it was more touch and go. With her finely chiseled Scandinavian facial features you could tell she had been a very pretty young woman. Now, she looked wary as if she didn't quite trust people, watching out for herself first. Perhaps it was her marcelled hair and her homemade dress that made me wish she'd spend more money on herself. Maybe it was the suitcase full of old kitchen pots and pans she'd brought us that made me sense her parsimonious nature. (That is not to say that she and Pop were not generous with us. We bought sterling silver—with an engraved monogram designed by Bob, settings for eight with a half dozen serving pieces, with the $200 wedding check they gave us.) Like many immigrants, they seemed inordinately proud of becoming Americanized. Although they thought they had none, I loved their Nordic accents. By the time we left for lunch I had become more at ease with them and knew that I could learn to love my dear husband's parents.

The Gables looked soft and misty in the rain as we approached along the tree-lined winding path to the main house with its encircling porch. Imagine our disappointment when we realized there were no cars in the parking lot, no sign of activity anywhere. Obviously, they were closed for lunch. We sat in the car pondering where we could go for lunch when suddenly Mrs. Townsend was standing on the porch waving us to come in. "I saw that beautiful big corsage and guessed the reason. Come in. Come in. It will only be a minute before we have luncheon ready for you." She seated us in a small dining room suited to the size of our party. Lighted candles on the table and buffet enhanced the Victorian setting and seemed to diminish the grayness of the sky. Softly from an unseen phonograph came the melded voices of Jeannette McDonald and Nelson Eddy singing "Oh, Happy, Happy Wedding Day"—just for us. The record played several times, and with each playing the words and melody seared themselves into our memory. The luncheon was perfect, complete with champagne and a decorated wedding cake adorned with a ceramic bride and groom on top.

Did I mention that Mom and Pop were to leave by plane at three thirty? When Bob looked at his watch and saw there was barely time to get his folks to the airport, a brief look of panic crossed his face. Mrs. Townsend accepted our heartfelt, but hurried, expressions of thanks and we dashed in the rain to Hank's car for a wild ride to the airport.

The acres of the flooded airport parking lot were almost empty. It was a good thing no one was in our way. Bob hydroplaned across that lot as he made sure his parents did not miss their flight. We sighed as we waved our good-byes as the plane lifted and headed for LaGuardia. Bob and I were glad they came, but happy now to be together...just the two of us.

This is not the whole story of the entire day of our wedding, but it's enough for you to see a bit of the beginning of a fifty-year love affair, a love that lasted until death did us part.

♄

A UNIQUE MIND

It took my husband five years of daydreaming to get a high school diploma. Constitutionally unable to learn what he wanted to know by sitting in a classroom, Bob compensated for that disability with unique talents for keen observation and independent thinking. He was smart and hardworking, but it was difficult for him to deal with second hand knowledge. It was not so much that he questioned authority as it was that he questioned the logic and the accuracy of the facts those in authority proffered.

Bob was an original do-it-yourselfer. Where others might turn to a book or an expert, Bob would apply his own skills and talents to solve a problem or answer a question. His interests were far ranging, from the function of a curve to the elimination of the income tax without increasing consumption taxes.

Bob Hansen, circa 1947

He may have flunked English Literature, but he loved reading Shakespeare: he had no need for a grade on a report card to validate his love for The Bard. The first person we visited when he took me to his home town was his English teacher: although she could never justify giving him high marks, she greeted him with warm affection.

It is not an easy thing to have Bob's kind of mind. It doesn't fit the mold of American culture. Certainly it didn't give him the grade points to attend an Ivy League college. Which was, of course, the least of his concerns. Nor did it guarantee him a position in the corporate world. That would have been the death of his own distinctive creativity. But he liked being who he was; no guilt, no excuses, no regrets.

Unlike his only sibling, Charles, who went to college and was an officer in the army during World War II, Bob chose to be a conscientious objector. It was not a hard decision for him to make: thou shalt not kill. Period. He accepted the consequences of his unpopular decision without rancor, serving his time in civilian public service as an aide in the violent ward of a mental institution. Without envy, greed or hate to occupy his thoughts and time, he was a singularly free man.

It never occurred to Bob to go along to get along. Except for repairing a roof or rescuing a kitten, his mind was uncluttered with thoughts of climbing ladders for success. This gave him freedom for creativity—and for fun.

Bob often found comedy by taking a precise, literal view of life around him. I didn't know all this about him when we married, but I did have some clues.

Shopping one night in downtown Detroit, we purchased an ashtray. Later, walking down the bright, crowded street to catch a bus, Bob lighted a Lucky Strike. As onlookers either smiled or suppressed a grin, Bob—in an outrageously ostentatious manner—flicked cigarette ashes into the ashtray. Not a big thing, but whenever I think of it, the scene is always in cartoon format.

I know now that when making pancakes the cook eats the first one. Either the griddle is too hot or too cold and the pancake comes off either burnt or soggy. Crispy black and brown was the first pancake I made as a married woman. As I tried unobtrusively to hide it from Bob's view, he started toward the door saying, "I'll be back in a minute." Back he came as promised with a nail and hammer he had borrowed from the janitor. Just as unobtrusively he tacked that first pancake to the wall! There it hung with its crags and crevices like an original sculpture in bas-relief.

Perhaps I should have shed tears, wailing that my husband was making fun of my cooking. But I couldn't. I laughed. Instead of being an insult to me, it made light of a potential domestic tragedy. That funny pancake adorned a wall in our breakfast nook until it begged to be discarded.

And so it is. Observing a unique mind or a pancake on a wall, love is in the eye of the beholder.

♭

Bob and Dorothy, circa 1979

A KEEN OBSERVER

An incident that illustrates the true nature of the one-and-only Bob Hansen and, one which shows how my life was enriched by him, is a time we were returning from a long trip to see Bob's parents in Florida.

It was in July of 1953 when Pop called to tell us that Bob's mother had taken a bad fall and was hospitalized near their home in Miami. Without hesitation, we hurriedly packed a few things, filled up the gas tank in our old Oldsmobile, and the three...almost four...of us headed east from California. Bob, anxious about his mother, our firstborn Johnny, 21 months old, the new baby, due to be born in a couple of weeks, and I, big and ungainly, covered the three thousand miles in record time. We stayed long enough for Mom to know we cared and for her to be back at home with good prospects for a complete, if not rapid, recovery. The active life inside me insisted on a speedy return to our home in Manhattan Beach and the availability of the nearest Kaiser hospital.

We were on the last and hottest day of our journey, traveling on Highway 10 from Blythe to Indio to Palm Springs to home. With no air conditioning in the car, we rode with the windows open, the hot air bearable only because of its brisk slapping on our skin as we sped along the flat desert highway. With the sun overhead, the macadam was at the boiling point and brief visions of mirages disappeared as we came closer to them. Some distance ahead, on the right hand shoulder of the road, we saw a man running, running with an urgency that defied the heat. He gripped something in his right hand. Was it a rope, or a belt?

As we passed him, we could see that it was a black man, a very dark-skinned man, with perspiration pouring over his slick and shiny skin. He was dressed in work pants and an old-fashioned "tank top" undershirt (the kind my husband wore) which was dripping with sweat. Although the man had not put out his thumb, it was no surprise to me that Bob pulled to a stop and offered him a ride.

Johnny scooted over so the man could get in the back seat behind me. With deep, heavy breaths, he panted, "Thank you, thank you." Still gripping the object in his hand, he held it up for Bob to see. It was a broken fan belt. With a minimum of words, he explained he was trying to get to his mother's funeral in Los Angeles and he'd left his family in the car while he struck out to find a replacement fan belt. They had driven straight through from Louisiana with no trouble until they were stranded in the desert. He was quiet then as we anxiously searched for a roadside garage. Ten or fifteen miles later we saw the cluster of shanties identified by a crudely printed sign as Desert Center. The sign touted a garage and cafe, but from the appearance of the enterprise, we would have passed it by were it not for the urgency of the man from Louisiana and the unlikelihood of finding any place at all, much less a better place, within miles.

The Desert Center garage had the right fan belt, and while our rider made his purchase, Bob bought chilled soft drinks and snacks for all, including the man's family. Bob turned the car around. When the man came from the garage, new fan belt in hand, Bob said to him. "We'll get you back to your car." The man shook his head. "No. You've done more than enough. I can hitch a ride." Bob reached over to open the door for him. "There's no time to wait for that to happen. C'mon, let's go." We drove back to his wife whose tears of relief touched the corners of her smile. The man gently shooed his three little kids from his knees as he set about replacing the fan belt.

We waved our good-byes as they opened their bottles of Dr. Pepper, Delaware Punch and Coca Cola.

We arrived in Manhattan Beach with weeks to wait for the arrival of Thomas Carl Hansen into our family. It was on the third trip to Kaiser that he made his welcomed earthly appearance.

Later, we wondered if the man we picked up in the desert reached his mother's funeral on time. I asked Bob how he judged when to pick up a hitchhiker, how he knew that man was okay. Bob shrugged. "It's obvious," he said. "I saw an old car parked on the shoulder. Its hood was up. A woman and some kids were in it. Then I saw the man running desperately...in that heat...with a broken fan belt in his hand. That family needed help. If someone needs help, you do what you can." Bob's keen observations made his decisions seem easy.

Bob was a man who lived freedom. Willing to take risks for others, not afraid to get involved, confident to meet the future, Bob, an unrepentant former Lutheran and avowed agnostic, without knowing it, held the Quaker view that "way will open." He helped to liberate me: I became less fearful, less timid, more sure of my decisions, kinder...all good things when faced with living alone. Happy memories help, too.

♄

THE LOT MAN

When we lived at 1514 Gates in Manhattan Beach, Bob studied to become a real estate agent, and soon left his job at Krienke's Appliances. By the time we moved to Third Street he was a licensed agent. To comply with California law, he was obliged to work for a broker for a specific period of time (I think it was two years). He didn't like working in an office full of agents vying for the potential house buyers as they walked in the door, so he found a broker that let him work on his own.

Bob specialized in sales of undeveloped property. Manhattan Beach, a desirable coastal community, had ready buyers who were eager to purchase lots for new homes. The difficulty was finding sellers willing to sell. During the week Bob researched ownership of vacant lots in the area, inspected the properties, and established a suggested selling price based on comparable values. He then set up a schedule of owners living in a specific outlying area—such as San Fernando—and, on Saturday when owners would most likely be at home, he made cold calls. Although unannounced, he generally was warmly greeted: no one expected an agent to come so far to make a call, Bob gave them up-to-date information that was useful to them, and he applied no pressure to sell. "When you're ready to sell, I'd appreciate your call." And they did...sometimes after he'd made several calls over a span of a couple of years. If he didn't already have a buyer, a small advertisement would produce good results. Bob supported the family and built a reputation as "The Lot Man."

Being "The Lot Man" suited Bob. There was less that could go wrong, and for those things that could mess up, he was prepared. He kept meticulous records and could vouch for zoning, percolation, or flooding facts. He preferred to show low lying property during a heavy rain storm: he didn't like for a buyer to be surprised. He often worked on verbal listings taking the risk that a seller could change his mind about selling, or could sell it on his own. In most instances, he found people trustworthy: a handshake being as good as a written document. Sometimes, though, he misjudged.

One instance I remember: Bob brought a seller an offer on her house that met all of her requirements. She looked it over, said she'd like to think about it overnight. When he checked with her the next day, she had gone around Bob to the buyers and made a deal with them directly, cutting Bob out of his commission. When he told her she had violated the trust he had in her, she responded, "I know what's right. I go to church."

Bob didn't change his ways. He never labored over his losses. The percentage of trust-worthy people far outweighed the ones who cheated. He'd say, "On to the next."

Often, it seems to me, real property transactions bring out the worst in people. Thinking of selling their home, owners suddenly view it as a mansion and believe it to be worth far more than its actual value. In a rational world, sellers might, before setting an asking price, allow for the dollar value for the time actually lived in their house instead of paying rent somewhere else—or, for that matter, the value of the enjoyment they have had living there. Many buyers look for potential resale value before considering a home's suitability to their lifestyle. With everyone—sellers, buyers, brokers, banks, escrow companies—focusing on the dollar sign, real estate deals can often degenerate into ulcer-creating conflicts or even legal battles.

In the twenty-five years Bob was in the real estate business, no complaint was ever filed against him.

After Bob had fulfilled the required two years working under a licensed broker, he became a broker and continued to work from his office (picnic table in the dining room) at home. He liked the flexibility of his hours, the short commute, and having meals with the family. An independent man, he liked being his own boss.

When we moved to Santa Rosa in 1959, I suggested to Bob that it might be worthwhile to work with an established broker. He thought it might work, that it would help him learn local customs more quickly. After some research, he offered his services to a broker who was delighted to put him to work. The next morning Bob set out with a list of the homes for sale through Multiple Listing which the broker had given him, and with a brand new Thomas Guide, the street guide and directory for Sonoma County, to familiarize himself with the properties and prices of real estate currently for sale. He planned to put in a full day, saying he'd be home in time for dinner.

I was surprised to see him park in the driveway at lunchtime. He came in, put his brief-case on the table, and announced, "That's it." "What do you mean, that's it" "Just...that's it. I can't work for someone else. I have my own way of doing things, my own ethics. That's the way I am."

The way he was made me proud and happy... but not rich. Bob continued to specialize in sales of unimproved properties, under the names of "5% Realty" (an unsuccessful experiment to increase volume by reducing commissions by 1%), and later as "E Street Real Estate."

The purchase of the lot at #2 E Street in Santa Rosa, the building of the mostly glass office building that withstood the earthquake of 1969, and its transformation to headquarters for R&D Products in 1976, are stories to be told on another day

♮

E Street Real Estate, circa 1969

THE ORIGINAL CALIFORNIA KOOK

One foggy winter's day in Manhattan Beach, Mrs. Barnett grunted to me through the open window that connected our kitchen to her backyard. "Here's soup," she said, in her own inimitable, inarticulate way. With all the politeness I could muster I thanked her and took the blackened pot from her hands. As I turned away from her I set it on the stove and hoped she would not see my expression of disgust. She had wandered into her garden, so I was safe. How could I get her to stop giving me food? I would keep it for a day or two before I threw it out. Then I had to scrub the pot and think how I could fake a favorable comment about it: "Oh, it was such delicious pea (or beef with barley, or lentil) soup, and Bob just loved it." She rarely saw Bob, so I could get by with that. I would stay out of the kitchen as much as I could, but the time would come when she'd be right there and I'd be forced into my little white lie as I handed the pot out the window to her.

What else could I do? She was our landlady. Down deep I knew she was doing the best she knew to be kind, especially since I was now obviously pregnant, but I have to tell you she was the original California kook. A 1951 variety of the stereotypical hippie with pirate loop earrings hanging below a head wrapped tight in a dirty, dingy, formerly brightly colored scarf. A blondish fuzz covered her wrinkled face on which I never saw a scintilla of a smile. No bra for her. Long, straggly underarm hair poked out from the sweat dampened sleeveless knit blouse she wore.

Both her blouse and skirt—which was usually an old but beautiful Scottish wool tweed wraparound fastened with a huge ornamental brass safety pin—were worn wrong side out.

In 1951 it was de rigueur for fastidious women to shave their legs, but Mrs. Barnett was neither fastidious nor shaven. Her hairy legs melded into feet that were unstockinged, unkempt, and ugly. She wore Birkenstocks before they were invented: her sandals were a homemade version that at best kept the soles of her feet somewhat safe from the poop of her precious Pekinese.

That doggy, with its long champagne colored hair held back by a perky pink bow, was part of the reason Bob and I never ate Mrs. Barnett's soup. Although I never actually saw her feed the dog from the ladle she used to stir the soup, it was a possibility. She held that dog in her arms most of the time, smooching it all the while. The very thought of soup flavored with dog hairs and dog saliva turned my already queasy stomach into big time nausea.

Mrs. Barnett cooked out of doors, not on a brick barbecue or a Weber grill, but on a regular kitchen stove installed on the cemented area just beyond my kitchen window. No sink or source of water was nearby, but every meal, rain or shine, she prepared there. From certain spots in my kitchen, I could surreptitiously watch her acts of defiance of all the rules of cleanliness and hygiene. Although I felt guilt ridden to throw out her well-meant gifts and then fib about it, I am proud to say I protected by husband and myself from who knows what—e-coli, salmonella, even sudden death.

Mrs. Barnett lived at that same address until she died at age ninety-four of nothing more than old age.

♄

HABITATS FOR THE HANSENS

Remembering our family life from the perspective of the different places we've lived gives a sharper image to the memories. I can see the smashed banana on the highchair tray, on grubby fat fingers, and smeared on terry bibs as each of you learned to eat solid food. The high chair sat in the space between the kitchen and the end of the dining table making feeding and cleanup equally efficient. A well-made redwood picnic table with benches served as our dining table, work table and crafts table. A picnic table in the dining room wasn't the fashion, but I loved the wood and the feel of that table. It suited our "style."

Exploiting the potential of our first home purchase, Bob and I set about making the house at 1544 Third Street in Manhattan Beach more livable. One of the first projects was to open the dining room to the patio by cutting a hole into the south wall. That was no small task as the house was built of cement blocks. Bob liked hard projects, and we enjoyed the result of his work when the Dutch door was installed.

I can visualize the dining room with its muslin cafe-curtained, paned windows opening to the morning sun and to the West's house. (All I remember about the West family is that Mrs. West had a very dull hobby: she mitered corners of the pages of Sears catalogs to form a free standing "sculpture." Mr. West left the keys in their car with the car pointed streetward so they could make a quick getaway in an emergency. The overhang from the big tree in their backyard served as shade for your tree house.). The dining room seemed larger than its true size as it was an open ell off the living room. With its new Dutch door, wood paneled wainscoting, and large oak-framed print of Peter Bruegel's "Children's Games," the dining room was a good beginning in making the house fit our family. I'll say more about the house later, but now...

Back to the bananas. They were a regular part of your early childhood diet. Bob had a penchant for bananas, you know, with his lunchtime ritual of a whole wheat bread sandwich with a banana broken in half on top of chunky peanut butter. I think it was Adele Davis's advice, not Bob's, that you each had a banana a day. Adele Davis was the health food guru in Southern California in the fifties, and I was an ardent follower. Each of you was breast fed for at least six months, and were weaned from the breast to Adele's Tiger's Milk, a high protein mixture that included evaporated milk and hefty portions of brewer's yeast.. Now as I think of it, wouldn't it have been nice of me if I'd flavored it with a bit of vanilla? You were remarkably healthy and much admired by our Kaiser pediatrician in San Pedro.

Dr. Schwartz was his name. We were members of Kaiser Permanente Health Plan by virtue of being members of the co-op in Santa Monica. We took you to San Pedro, their closest clinic, for your well baby-exams. Bob and I both went, partly because of my aversion to driving and partly because that's the way we liked to do things. We thought Dr. Schwartz was a wonderful doctor: he bragged on our parenting and your good health. We strutted as we left the clinic, feeling proud of ourselves. It was many, many well-baby exams later, as we sat in a cubicle waiting for the doctor that we overheard him telling the parent in the adjacent cubicle the very same stuff he told us.

As was typical of family in the 1950s, Daddy went off to work in the morning and came home at night to find the house clean, dinner ready, and children nurtured by Mom. But our family was not typical in that you were not Dad deprived.

♄

LIFE AFTER DEATH

Bob's mother, Helga Larsen Hansen, had an automatic weapon she used to get her way. She could make herself sick at will. She kept her husband tightly reined with her cleverly feigned illnesses. Her two sons, however, reacted differently. The eldest and her favorite, Charles, was an apt student and practitioner of her techniques of control. Her second son, my husband, Bob, matter-of-factly accepted her as she was and escaped the squinty-eyed life of a manipulator. Even so, the time came when Bob became a cooperative victim of Helga's schemes.

Bob's mother and father retired to Miami, Florida, shortly after Bob and I were married in 1948. Coming to America from Norway when they were in their teens—Mom as a housemaid and Pop as a ship's carpenter—they met in a Lutheran church in Brooklyn, married, and lived in New Jersey among family and friends from Norway. Pop became a successful independent building contractor, specializing in fine homes in good neighborhoods in and around Leonia.

Helga, Carl, Dorothy holding Paul, Tom and John., circa 1956

In Miami, he built a large house on a waterway in which he and Mom lived a comfortable life of retirement for over twenty years. Their circumstances changed when the city, under power of eminent domain, took their property for public use. Pop, in his mid-seventies, eagerly designed and started construction on a new home.

The house was nearing completion when, without forewarning, he died in his sleep. Helga buried her husband, and without skipping a beat, worked with contractors to complete the house and sell it.

Her plan, which she had not disclosed to the affected parties, was to move to Palo Alto and live with one or more of her four sisters who had settled there. Our home was not among her choices for a domicile, perhaps because our lifestyles were not in harmony, but most likely because Bob was not easily controlled. It wasn't long before her sisters decided they would gladly help her find a place to live as long as it was not in their own homes.

It was then Helga got sick and called Bob. "Mom," he told her. "You're welcome to come here."

We looked at each other and gulped. Although we had talked of caring for her at some future time, we knew having her now was asking for trouble.

Eager for our three sons—twelve, fourteen and sixteen—to have a living-in-the-country experience before it was too late, we had just stretched our fiscal limits to purchase twenty-three acres on Olivet Road, four miles west of Santa Rosa, California. The tumble-down shack on the property wasn't in livable condition, but we decided to live there anyway. We could tolerate it, we rationalized, while building a proper house. As a native Oklahoman, I had misgivings about living in stereotypical Okie shambles, even temporarily, but it was an adventure and we were having fun. Just how Okie was it? The dining area, in one corner of the main room, had a dirt floor with an outdoors water faucet sticking up through the dirt. The room where Bob and I slept was wall-to-wall bed, and we attached an old chicken house to the shack to make a dormitory for the boys. Helga had good reason to put us at the bottom of her list.

However, being the center of attention, she recovered quickly from her illness. She didn't like living in the country: she liked being close to stores. She had no interest in tumbling pigeons, sheep, rabbits, or a gaggle of geese...and very little in her grandsons. She had lost interest in embroidery, and she didn't like to read.

When Bob came home from work each day (he had a real estate office in downtown Santa Rosa) she pestered him about when he was going to make his next sale, a nagging designed to quash interaction. Life with us was dull for her, and, for us, her presence palled our enthusiasm for living in the country. Easy days were hard to come by.

We often ate our meals outdoors under the welcoming shade of a magnificent oak tree with a canopy of leafy branches one hundred feet wide. At one particular lunchtime, the geese were making a nuisance of themselves. Mom really didn't care for them and they knew it. They kept trying to peck at her flowered dress. Annoyed, she got up to go inside. No sooner had she risen than the biggest of the geese goosed her right at the center of a well-placed flower. I was very proud of our sons for swallowing their sniggers.

Mom was not happy at our house. So she asked me to give her an enema. I had never given anyone an enema and told Bob that I was a little nervous about it. Without a word, he went to his Mom and told her we would share what we had with her, we would feed her and do the best we could to care for her, but that she was not to ask me to give her an enema. "If you need an enema, we'll make an appointment for you to go to a doctor's office to get one." She gave us the silent treatment, and I gave Bob my everlasting love.

The next day we had a call from Gertie, one of Mom's sisters in Palo Alto. She reported that she had received a phone call from Mom's neighbor in Florida. (We had met the neighbor when we visited there. She was a woman, herself in poor health, who was caring for her ninety-year-old mother who lived with her.) Panicked, the neighbor told Gertie that Helga had called her saying she was coming to Florida to live with her. And she was going to do it right away.

I felt sorry for Mom. Here she was, essentially homeless, widowed and rejected. She had not taken time to grieve for Pop, or to think how to build her new life without him. How could she have the nerve to impose herself on her former neighbor? Bob and I talked about what we might do, and all we could think of was to call Josephine Deyo for advice. Josephine was a social worker who worked mostly with the elderly. I didn't know her well, but what I knew I liked. When I called, she listened carefully to my sad story. I told her that I couldn't stand the thought of Mom's being rejected again.

She asked me, "Is Bob's mother competent?"

"What do you mean 'competent'?"

"Can she reconcile her checkbook?"

"Can she ever!" I replied.

Josephine counseled me. "You must let her go to Florida. She will be rejected by her neighbor. She may get sick or be hospitalized. You cannot make her decisions for her. You should make clear to her what you can offer her, but you should not move into town. You should not try to fill her husband's shoes. You cannot replace him. No matter what you do, it will never be enough." Josephine's predictions came true. We put Mom on a plane to Florida. The next we heard she called us from a hospital.

Her sisters agreed to help her find a place in Palo Alto. With the aid of Little House, a senior services center, she lived for a year or so sharing a home with a man about her age. They ate together, played cards, and Mom said she locked her door when she went to her bedroom for the night. Later she shared a sunshiny apartment a short walk from Little House with Pansy, a flighty little lady whose fading memory produced malapropisms worth making the two hour drive from Santa Rosa to Palo Alto just for the laughs. Mom had made a life for herself.

Without my expecting it, Mom has been an inspiration to me in these, my widowed years.

FIRSTBORN SON

Several hours before dawn on this day fifty years ago—October 1, 1951—I looked into the mirror and watched, spellbound, as my firstborn left my body to begin life on his own. I lay under the bright lights of the delivery room at White Memorial Hospital in Los Angeles where a large mirror, perhaps five feet square, was hung from the ceiling and tilted appropriately so that I could observe the miracle of birth as a white-clad, masked doctor expertly assisted in the perfectly normal birth of John Dale Hansen. My dreams had come true, but I wanted to hear that first lusty cry as the doctor carefully held him head down. Instead, my son John announced his arrival in this world by peeing all over the place.

Dorothy with infant John, circa 1951

Quickly, Johnny was taken away, cleaned and weighed (seven and a half pounds) and put into the nursery. After making a few stitches (episiotomies were usual, I was told, especially with first births), the doctor congratulated me and nurses rolled me onto a gurney and out of the delivery room to a hall near the maternity ward. There I was left with other new mothers who were waiting for a room: there had been a rash of deliveries that night and space and staff were at a premium. The spinal block which had allowed a painless birth and the drugs used to sedate me left me dry mouthed. Never had I wanted a drink of water so badly. Nurses were tending to everyone but me, or so I felt, and they didn't bring me either a drink or my baby. It was several hours before I was placed in a room where I received normal care.

Bob was not there with me. About midnight he was told to go home to get some rest, as, after several hours of intense labor pains, an unyielding cervix kept the baby inside.

Bob made the trip home from the hospital which was in Boyle Heights, Los Angeles, to our apartment in Manhattan Beach, a good hour's drive. He was exhausted: this having a baby was tough work. It began the day before, early in the afternoon, when I started labor. Since it was a long drive to the hospital we left before the contractions were close, but before we arrived I was definitely down to business. Bob sat by my side in the crowded labor room trying with sweet love to comfort me as the contractions were more and more intense and the time between was less and less. Illogically, I believed that labor would be more bearable if I had a hamburger and chocolate malt. With the nurse's permission, he went out to Big Boy's to bring the food I craved. I gratefully devoured it. That was, as the nurse and Bob and I soon realized, a dumb thing to do. The cleanup was not pleasant.

Bob had crashed on the sofa as soon as he arrived at our apartment. After a few hours of restless sleep, he called the hospital and was told I had delivered. When he asked what I had delivered the nurse officiously chirped, "I'm not allowed to give you that information over the phone." Frustrated, anxious, he jumped into our old reliable Oldsmobile and headed for L.A. He didn't make it there: the car conked out in Inglewood, refusing to budge. Unfamiliar with the public transit system, he finally found a bus to take him into the city. The bus stopped near Brentano's and he had a half hour before his transfer bus to Boyle Heights was to leave. He used that time to buy a boxed four book set of A. A. Milne's "Winnie the Pooh" for his son or daughter—whichever.

By the time Bob arrived at the hospital, I had nursed my son and had inspected him thoroughly. He was almost perfect. But it seemed to me that his left foot turned in more than the right. I needed to ask Bob about that.

There was very little getting-acquainted time before the nurse took my baby away. Tired but happy, I napped for a while. An affectionate tweak of my toes told me Bob was standing at the foot of my bed. "Well, is it a boy or a girl?"

The nurse brought Johnny back and we marveled at our creation. Just what our hearts desired. Bob agreed that his little left foot did turn in a bit and suggested I ask the doctor about it when he made his daily visit. The staff was helpful and brought in an orthopedist who diagnosed it as a mild club foot. He demonstrated several massage exercises that I was to perform with every diaper change. He told me to bring the baby in for a checkup in nine weeks.

Although I, with three younger siblings, should have known about babies (Bob had never cared for an infant) guess who, when Johnny had the hiccups the very afternoon we brought him home, called excitedly, "Where's Dr. Spock?" Bob patiently brought me the book, but by that time the hiccups were gone.

Marriage with baby was a soul satisfying and sleep deprived condition. I never nursed Johnny when I was lying in bed for fear of falling asleep and rolling over on him. My maternal instinct was at its blissful peak as I sat in the rocking chair nursing that precious hunk of humanity, drinking milk and nibbling on a cracker to keep myself awake.

Intensely, conscientiously, I massaged that little left foot as a part of the routine of diaper changing, in the wee hours of the night and as many times a day as it took. When the nine weeks were up, we dutifully took Johnny in for his checkup. White

Memorial was a teaching hospital so the doctor stood in the front of the classroom demonstrating to his students the exercises he had prescribed. Then, to show how the work I had done had straightened Johnny's foot and spine, he held my naked little one by his heels, and you know what? Johnny pissed all over him. That's my John. I've loved him all these fifty years, and I don't think I'll stop.

JULIA'S PREDICAMENT

I did not expect to come back from my father's funeral in Norman, Oklahoma, with a commitment to participate in a deceitful scheme.

It was December 1951. Bob and I lived in Manhattan Beach, California, with our firstborn. Johnny was only nine weeks old, but when the call came that Daddy had died of a stroke, it was only hours before Bob put us on a plane to Oklahoma. I stayed several days beyond the date of the funeral. I wanted to be of what comfort I could to Mother, and, of course, I liked showing off my perfect child to all the family.

The day before I was to return, my sister Mary asked me to come alone with her to meet someone. I wondered why "alone," why "someone." Why all the mystery? I shrugged it off, thinking she might have arranged some little surprise for me. I could never have guessed what she had in mind.

I left Johnny in Mother's capable care. As we drove across town Mary told me about the person she wanted me to meet and the reason for the meeting. Although it had to do with Mary's job as a social worker with the Oklahoma State Department of Adoptions where she had been employed for about fifteen years, I was not prepared for what it would mean to me.

Mary pulled into a parking space at a modest motel on the south side of town. We walked to the end of the first floor corridor. Mary knocked lightly on the door of the last unit. The door opened and we were silently invited in by an attractive but somber young girl.

"Julia," Mary said. "This is my sister Dorothy from California. She's here to help you." We found seats, Mary on the bed, Julia sat on the desk chair, and I pulled up the arm chair for myself. Mary had brought a thermos of coffee. She lighted a cigarette after Julia and I shook our heads to her offer. Mary's knack for being laid back and in charge at the same time made it easy for me to learn Julia's dilemma.

Julia looked like a nice girl from a good family. She must have been about nineteen, with the healthy, shiny hair of youth, and a well-groomed style that suggested good taste and good upbringing. Dressed in a wool plaid shirt, cashmere pullover and matching cardigan, no one would know she was pregnant. She could not tell her parents. She loved her parents too much to disgrace them with having a child out of wedlock. They were outstanding citizens in the small farm town near Oklahoma City where they and their parents before them lived. Mary had learned enough about Julia's situation to concur that her parents must never know.

Mary knew a licensed place where Julia could live during her pregnancy and until her baby was adopted. She could then go home in the shape she left it. All that was needed was for someone to help her pretend that she was living a carefree life in...maybe California. I then agreed to send a letter to Julia each week, telling her the news (earthquakes, etc.) about southern California. The plan we plotted was that she would send me an envelope in which she had placed a letter to her parents or friends which I would then mail to them.

Each week for many months I pretended to be Julia, a newcomer to California, writing how the fog hung heavy late into the day, how the palm trees and the beaches were just like the postcards, how casual the people were, how life was great in the Golden State. Sometimes I sent newspaper clippings, anything to make the letters she wrote more believable. Her parents received letters from her with the return address 1514 Gates, Manhattan Beach, telling of her adventures in California.

One afternoon I answered a knock at my door. A stranger, a middle-aged woman with an Oklahoma twang, asked for Julia, and explained she was visiting relatives in Los Angeles and Julia's mother had asked her to bring some things for Julia. For a moment, I felt so grateful for the presence of a gentle Oklahoman, I was about to invite her in. Then I remembered I was a coconspirator in this deceit. My body stiffened. I'm not good at lying. I told her Julia no longer lived here.

"Do you have her new address?"

"No"

"How long ago did she move?"

I glared at her. "I don't care to talk about it." As if Julia and I had parted on bad terms. The bewildered lady turned and walked to her car.

After I calmed down, I called my sister. Somehow Mary and Julia worked it out. Julia's healthy baby was born and adopted. I do not know if she successfully kept the truth from her parents. For myself, I am not sure if the deceit really helped.

In the past half century, some of the strict social customs about births out of wedlock have changed. Perhaps today Julia could tell her parents....and they could face the facts and welcome the child with love.

♭

THIRD TIME'S THE CHARM: HERE COMES TOM

It was a long distance call from Florida. Pop asked to talk with Bob. I could tell something was wrong. He was calling from a hospital, said Mom slipped on a grape, fell down hard on their tiled kitchen floor, and the doctor said she had a bad break in her hip. She was in the operating room and he was just waiting so he thought to call us and let us know. There was no question in Bob's mind. We should go there immediately to give his parents our support.

At that time, in mid-June, 1953, we lived across the country from them in Manhattan Beach, California. That night Bob notified Ollie Krienke, his boss at Krienke Appliances, that he would not be at work for a couple weeks. We packed our things, sent a wire to Mom and Pop, and early the next morning the three of us—Bob and Johnny, our twenty-two-month old, and I—piled in our big, old Oldsmobile sedan and headed east. We had another passenger, as yet invisible, who came with us.

Nine months pregnant with a restless fetus in my womb, I was a bit apprehensive about those three thousand miles ahead of us. The tumbling motions and vigorous, insistent kicks I felt were strong signals to me that the healthy somebody inside would soon demand more attention. I worried that we would not be back in California by the predicted end-of-June due date. Bob saw to it that we made a quick trip to Miami.

One thing about Bob, whatever task he had ahead, he just did it. Driving seven or eight hundred miles a day in an old car, so? Missing sleep, so? As rushed as we were, we were happy on the road. Why shouldn't we be?

We were in our early thirties, healthy, easy with each other, and very much in love. Our precious Johnny brought us added pleasure, being cute and happy and sleeping well as we rolled over the miles. And the squirmy one inside was still inside where I hoped he would stay for a few more weeks.

By the time we arrived in Miami, Pop had the situation well under control and Mom's hip was healing appropriately. There wasn't much we could do except to show we cared. We stayed a few days so Johnny could have some grandparent time, then we left hot and humid Miami and started the trip home. But there was a big problem.

We could not possibly drive across the country and not stop in Oklahoma to see my family. Mother lived in Norman so we drove there where sisters Pat and Mary and Ann joined us. Each day I was getting more and more nervous as I got bigger and bigger and bigger. Mother's doctor examined me and she didn't see any reason why I couldn't make the rest of the trip without mishap. It was a shortened visit with my folks because I was still anxious and ready to go home. Our car had no air-conditioning and the weather was insufferably hot. Our route took us through Phoenix. To get there we had to drive through the Red River Canyon on a narrow, twisty road that wound around the mountains in nonstop S-curves. The view may have been spectacular but all I could see was the precipitous drop at the edge of the road where one wrong move could catapult a car hundreds of feet to the bottom of the canyon. At that time, Arizona's highway department had the unnerving practice of marking the site of deadly accidents with a white cross for each fatality. The more crosses I saw the more taut were my nerves. Frequently we had to stop for construction crews with their massive earth-moving machines stirring up clouds of rust-colored dirt as they maneuvered at the very edges of the roads.

Foremost in my mind were thoughts of a recent accident, in conditions just like these, where my friends Marion and Ward Martin were seriously injured and laid up in a hospital far from home for weeks and weeks. I started to cry and to shake. I couldn't stop shaking. At no time in my life have I been so close to hysteria.

Bob stopped at the next vista point and we rested there while I—with Bob's gentle patience and support—gained better control of my feelings. We soon came quickly out of the mountains to the welcome flat land of Phoenix. Disheveled, covered with sweat and dust, we stopped at the first air conditioned restaurant we saw. I said to the waitress, "Thank Goodness. We made it. We just came across that treacherous Red Canyon road." "Oh?" she said, sounding surprised. "I travel that road twice a day to come to work."

Luckily, the baby was still inside when we arrived in Manhattan Beach. Exhausted, I sat on the front porch that evening absorbing the balmy coolness of the moist ocean air. I sat. And the next day, I sat. And sat. And sat, waiting for something to happen. Days passed.

One day when showering I thought my water broke. It was a long drive from our house to the hospital, so even though I was not having contractions, we took Johnny to stay with our good neighbor, Jenny Sporcic, and drove through the Los Angeles traffic into Hollywood to the Kaiser Hospital on Sunset Boulevard. I was admitted, put in a wheelchair and rolled to the labor room. Bob was not permitted to go with me, a custom which has fortunately changed. So he sat in the waiting room. He sat. And sat. All the while, at the doctor's instruction, I walked. He said it might help get the contractions going. I walked, and finally, Bob went home for the night. At the end of the next day, I was released from the hospital, disappointed not to have a baby in my arms.

The next week, same thing all over again, except that I shed some tears over my unproductive efforts. A doctor observed my crying and insensitively asked, "Why are you crying? There are some women in here with real pain, something real to cry about." Empty handed as I was, that doctor made me glad to go home that night.

Almost a week later, the contractions were stronger and closer together, but still in the beginning stages. The trip to the hospital was so long and the traffic unpredictable, but I did believe with all my heart that this time I would be successful. We took Johnny to Jenny's house again, put my bag in the car, and headed for Sunset Boulevard. We would just sit in the car in the hospital parking lot and not enter that labor room until the contractions were undeniable, and that we did. However, that labor room had a jinx on me: my contractions abated as soon as I admitted. All night I lay there sleepless, disappointed, exhausted, wondering what could be wrong. Almost three weeks beyond the due date, bigger than a barn, and being kicked constantly by that life inside, I was beginning to feel desperate. Minutes later, at least so it seemed, doctors were at my bedside telling me they had decided the best thing to do was to induce labor and they would start that process within the hour. At that point, I needed all the help I could get.

Wide awake now, I was put on a delivery table and hooked up to a couple of intravenous injection tubes (I believe one of the drugs was pituitrin). I watched as the doctors monitored the drugs' effect on my body, and I was keenly aware that we were getting down to business. It took a while, maybe an hour or two, and it was good hard work, but when a doctor held our new baby boy for me to see I was filled with love, and satisfaction, too. I was also exhausted.

Kaiser Hospital at that time had a unique set up in their maternity ward. The ward was designed so that the healthy newborns could be put into a well-padded specially built file drawer that could be pulled in one direction by the mother so she could have her baby with her immediately and for as long as she wished...with every opportunity to bond with the baby. When the mother wanted to rest, she would simply push the drawer back and the baby would then be safe and secure in the nurse's station.

It was there that Bob welcomed his son, Thomas Carl, into his heart. Together, with wonder and awe, we looked over all eight pounds twelve ounces of him, marveling at his soft reddish hair, his nice flat ears, his well-shaped head, and his healthy body. We could have sworn he was born with a smile on his face. We could not then have imagined what delight he would bring to our lives, but we hoped he could somehow sense how wanted, how loved he was.

Dorothy and Thomas, circa 1953

Home was a little house on a hill on Gates Avenue. When we brought Tommy home, we found a forlorn looking Johnny waiting on the front steps. He must have wondered when we had gone to the hospital for the third time if we were ever going to bring home his new little brother. The third time's the charm. Now we were four in our family—with the happy prospect of many a tale to tell.

♮

PAUL DAVID HANSEN IS BORN

*Letter to Clare and Ann on the Occasion of their
Father's 46th Birthday: July 16, 2001*

Dorothy holding Paul, approximately 6 mos, circa 1955

Parts, maybe all, of what I am about to say in this letter you may have already heard, but since you have asked me to write down some stories about family, it seemed to me that your father's birth might be a good place to start. Besides, when I awakened this morning I was thinking how busy your Dad and I were on this day forty-six years ago.

At that time, July 1955, we were living in Manhattan Beach, California, about fifteen blocks from the ocean. I awakened early that morning, even before the mockingbird announced another brand new day, knowing this was the day our third baby would be born. Just at dawn each morning for the past several weeks a loud, happy mockingbird sat on a high wire on the quiet street in front of our house and awakened me with repeated renditions of his full repertoire of mimicry. As I lay there struggling to find a comfortable position to accommodate that squirming bigness that was your dad inside of me, the mockingbird's song was a challenge to me. It told me, Pay attention to this day: be aware…

Now, as I waited for the mockingbird to begin his morning serenade, my senses were keen. I was conscious of everything about me: the softness of the early morning ocean air; the mingled fragrance of eucalyptus and roses and jasmine wafting through the open window; the changing of the light in our bedroom as dawn became day; the comfort, strength and sweetness of Bob lying next to me; and of the big-time action going on in my body. No urgent contractions, no frenetic movements inside, just a convincing pressure. Pay attention. Be aware. I was content as the mockingbird's song signaled a new and important day.

Bob suggested it was time we get ready for the long drive from Manhattan

Beach to the Kaiser Hospital on Sunset Boulevard in Hollywood. We had made that trip many times for doctor visits and when Tom was born two years ago, so we knew to expect heavy traffic. With my bag packed and gas in the car, we needed only to say our good-byes before leaving.

My mother had come from Oklahoma to help. It was her first visit to our home and to California: I think it was her first plane ride. Early as it was, we awakened her and Johnny and Tommy (yes, we called them by those diminutives back then) to tell them we were on our way. We didn't want the boys to awaken and find us gone without their knowing where we were.

The drive to the hospital was uneventful. Although definite, my contractions were not overly strong and Bob sensed I was more calm. I can't remember where we parked, or how far we had to walk to the hospital, but we must have thought we arrived prematurely for as soon as I was admitted, Bob left for a cup of coffee. He knew from experience that he would have plenty of time as I was in labor for twelve hours before John was born, and it took three trips to this same hospital plus induced labor for Tom to make his appearance. I told Bob to relax and enjoy his breakfast as the Pink Lady volunteer wheeled me to the labor room.

There a nurse helped me onto the examining table. As I lay down, I found myself letting out a surprised "WOW." I felt a down-to-business contraction. "Now take it easy," the nurse said. "Let's not get too excited." (I think she meant let's not get too noisy, but she didn't need to worry as I'm not the screaming type.)

She started to prep me for delivery when she immediately called out, "Doctor! Doctor!" in an urgent, demanding voice. Several doctors responded to her call and before I knew it, I was in the delivery room, doctors hovering over me, and contractions coming close and so strong I thought the baby would pop out instantaneously.

The doctors gave me a spinal block which desensitized the birth canal. Perhaps they also gave me a sedative, because I lay there hazily watching the doctors and feeling so blissful, thinking isn't it wonderful how modern medicine makes it possible for a woman to have a baby essentially without pain. (I thought of the night—I was ten years old—when my mother gave birth to my brother Jack and I sat on the front porch listening to the sounds coming from the bedroom where he was born.

Mother gave birth to nine children, all naturally, without benefit of pain medications. With the advent of effective anesthetics, few women gave birth naturally. A few years after Paul was born, the advantages of giving birth without anesthesia became so convincing that mothers were actually trained for natural child birth. I found a book, studied and exercised on my own, but that was before doctors advised or supported it. I felt lucky to be so free of pain. It was only later I learned that while I was filled with my sanguine thoughts, the doctors were frantically working to save your dad's life. The umbilical cord had twisted itself around his neck and the fear of his being choked to death was real and imminent.

My joy was complete. A third boy? No problem at all. Welcome to the Hansen household, Paul David. All nine pounds, two ounces of you. No wrinkly skin like a preemie, you looked perfect with your dark brown hair and eyes that were bluer than the L.A. sky...no, no, than a clear blue sky. All your parts in the right places, too.

As Bob says they say in Norway, "Ye err rundily fersinct." (I'll have to look up the spelling for that.) It means "I am roundly satisfied." And so I was.

But where was Bob?

In those days fathers were not allowed in the delivery room. The first that Bob saw of Paul was when I was rolled out of the delivery room with Paul, all clean and fresh and new lying in my arms. You know your grandpa. He looked at his healthy third-born son, and then at me, tenderly touching our cheeks with his big, strong hands, as he shed tears of love and joy. Your mother says, "Every child needs someone who's just wild about them." That's how we felt about your Dad. (And still do.)

♄

TIME FOR MISCHIEF

Breast feeding, I fantasized, is the quiet time for mother and child to bond, for mutual nurturing, a time for the dependent child to feel secure and loved and for the mother to pay close attention to this new life she has brought into the world—awestruck with the depth of her love and her willingness to accept the responsibility that such a love entails.

I say "I fantasized" because that vision doesn't describe what actually happened to me when I chose to breastfeed my sons. The love, the nurturing, and the wonder were there in abundance, but the "quiet time" was an illusion, more a goal than a fact.

With John, there were quiet times—in the middle of the night. Although I was 31 when he was born in October 1951, I sometimes felt as tentative as a teenage mother. When I heard the slightest sound from his bassinet near our bed, I eagerly lifted him into my arms and walked to the waiting rocking chair which I had set up before going to bed with a table nearby holding a thermos of milk, a glass, and a few graham crackers. Just as I would not nurse my baby in bed for fear of falling asleep and smothering him, I would not fall asleep in a chair and let him slip from my arms. Johnny nursed as we gently rocked and rocked. Peace surrounded us. Then, as my head descended forward ending with an abrupt jerk to wakefulness, I reached for the milk and crackers.

Daytime was different. It was hard to ignore the phone for it meant missing a call as there were no answering machines in those days, and it seemed the phone always rang when it was nursing time. I let it ring.

I juggled chores to accommodate a flexible nursing schedule. Overall, we managed pretty well until, at six months, I weaned him to Tiger's Milk, a concoction containing brewer's yeast advocated by nutrition guru Adele Davis. Johnny was off to a healthy start.

When Tommy was born twenty-two months later, there was no question about nursing him. I was an old hand at motherhood, but those longed-for quiet times to hold him close were more elusive. Like the telephone caller who knew just when to disturb us, Johnny's need for attention often coincided with Tommy's need for nourishment. Sometimes the three of us snuggled on the sofa. As Tommy nursed, Johnny listened to stories. Other times were less tranquil: I was pulled in two directions with Tommy at the breast and Johnny on the go. Although Bob's flexible work schedule and his parenting skills often rescued me from impinging disaster or depression, the self-imposed role of supermom took its toll. I often wished I'd met Bob when I was eighteen instead of twenty-eight...then I wouldn't be thirty-three years old and mothering two active, interesting, wonderful kids. Tommy had a full six months of mother's milk and then, like his brother, was weaned to Tiger's Milk.

Bob gave Tom his second birthday party as I was at Kaiser Hospital in Hollywood getting acquainted with Paul, who was born the day before, on July 16, 1955. I took advantage of my few hospital days to absorb the essence of Paul. I knew when we went home to 1544 Third Street in Manhattan Beach, time alone with him would be hard to schedule.

Try nursing a hungry baby with an inquisitive two year old and an independent almost-four year-old in your care. As soon as John and Tom detected Paul's Feed Me indicators, their sparkling eyes revealed their minds' automatic shift to "Now, what can we do that's really fun?"

On one occasion when I was nursing Paul, John scooted off unobserved. When I retrieved him from Johnny Swartz's house two doors down, I brought him home, scolded him, and sat him in the rocking chair facing the kitchen where I was working. After a while, scowling, he told me, "I know why you're so sour." I had my own reason, but his was, "You eat sour pickles."

Tommy climbed before he could walk. When he was just over a year old, I put him down for his afternoon nap making sure he was sound asleep before I left him and went to the kitchen to bake a cake. After a while I heard a soft sound at the back door, not a knock but like a kitten wanting to come in. It was Tommy with his big happy smile. He had climbed out of his crib, crawled to the open bedroom window, climbed over and out, and crawled to the back door where he proudly announced his presence. He was cute then, but those climbing skills increased with each new day and although I locked the outside doors when I nursed Paul, that did not deter Tommy. Bob put latches higher on the doors until the final ones were within inches of the top of the door.

Nursing time for Paul and me was mischief time for Johnny and Tommy. As I became more creative in cooperating with them and their hi-jinks, I relished the ingenuity of my bright, inventive sons. As a more seasoned mother, I no longer needed to be a supermom. I learned to find quiet times in the midst of mischief.

♄

THE SHINNY POLE

The shinny pole Bob put up in our backyard gave our three sons plenty of opportunity for good strength building exercise. I'm not sure how they managed to maneuver themselves up the twenty feet or so to the top where they, after they had got used to the idea of being able to stay up there, acknowledged their skill with wild displays of self-confidence. Hey, look at me was the general idea. The scariest part for me was when they locked their legs around the pole and slid down lickety-split to the ground.

The pole provided good exercise and built muscle coordination for sure, but it was fifty years later at the memorial service for Bob in February, 1999, that I learned its true value.

We lived in the "soil" section, fifteen blocks from the ocean in Manhattan Beach, California, when our three sons were born. The "sand" section, closer to the water or at least with a view of it, was the ritzier part of town where living the good life, Southern California style, was the purpose of being. There was a certain feeling if you lived in the Los Angeles area back in the 1950s that you were allowed to believe you lived every day at a vacation resort instead of in the real world. A Hollywood phoniness pervaded the atmosphere, even fifteen blocks from the ocean in Manhattan Beach.

One night, after the boys had their bedtime ritual of baths and stories and cod liver oil and were sound asleep in their beds, Bob and I talked about the possibilities for them in such an indulgent climate. How could they have everyday, ordinary experiences in a make-believe world?

We envisioned the future: three well-tanned, good-looking beach bums with their surf boards and boom boxes. That's the night we decided to move.

Very deliberately we set about to find a place which would provide a wide variety of real life experiences. After several trips to northern California we, like Luther Burbank who chose Sonoma County as the ideal spot as far as nature is concerned, chose it as the ideal spot to nurture our three sons into their maturity. We liked the easy access to the ocean, redwood forests, farms and orchards, combined with good schools, a feeling of community, diversity of climates and terrain, and having the resources of Berkeley and San Francisco only fifty miles away. We sold our house in Manhattan Beach and, in the summer of 1959, moved to new adventures in Santa Rosa.

Paul was four; Tom, six, and John was eight years old when we moved into the modest tract home in west Santa Rosa. The best thing about it was the open field behind it where Bob took the boys to look for arrowheads. They would go after a rain when the black obsidian glistened its location as if wanting to be found by some young child.

It was this kind of life we hoped for when we decided to move.

A few weeks after we were settled in, Bob went shopping for a twenty-foot metal pole and some cement. With some difficulty he dug a hole in the hard adobe soil in our backyard and anchored the pole securely into the hole as he filled it with cement. Waiting for the cement to dry was the hard part; shinnying up the pole seemed an easy, natural skill for each child. I did the worrying for the family, but I can't recall anything more than a few scratches or sore muscles from the shinny pole adventures.

Bob with John, Paul and Tom in backyard at Palomino Dr., Santa Rosa, CA, circa 1964

When Bob died, Paul was 44; Tom, 46; and John, 48. Among the comments made by family and friends about Bob at his memorial service was Tom's: "Dad wanted us to have a bigger view. He put up this shinny pole in the backyard, and I can tell you, hanging on up there, twenty or twenty-five feet up in the air with the pole sort of swaying back and forth, I got a different view of the neighborhood and the world."

♮

GENESIS OF R&D PRODUCTS, INC.

As essential as a journal to a writer, Bob's yellow ruled pads were always close by so he could jot down a note or make a drawing of an idea he didn't want to lose. Bob fastened a yellow ruled pad to his favorite clipboard. It was his only clipboard. Made of brown pressboard, the clipboard's lower left hand corner had been clunked at some earlier time leaving a raggedy edge. It wasn't pretty, but it had a strong bear-clasp that lay flat and held the pad securely. I never knew Bob to use another clipboard: it seems to me he had it when I first met him in 1948 and he still used it fifty years later.

Sometimes Bob wrote brief descriptions of ideas that came to him. His narrative style was telegraphic: no flowery adjectives. Just the facts. Most often there was a sketch with a date and an identifying name. The drawings were usually a cross section of an idea for a product. To me, cross section drawings were hieroglyphics. Unlike Bob, it was hard for me to visualize a physical item in that way. Bob filled pads of yellow ruled paper with sketches of cross sections which he would file for future reference.

Bob's head was full of surprises. It was no surprise to me when he called out as he came home for lunch one spring day in 1973, "Hey. I have an idea. Wanna look?"

Of course I wanted to look: I never knew what was coming from that brain of his. I was also interested in how his appointment with the escrow officer had gone that morning.

At that time Bob supported the family as the owner/broker of E Street Real Estate in Santa Rosa, California, and I wanted assurance there would be no delay in getting our commission from the sale that was in escrow. I waited as Bob eagerly pulled the yellow pad from his briefcase to show me his new idea. As it turned out, that new idea birthed at his morning's appointment and was more rewarding to us than any real estate commission could ever have been.

As I pushed aside the table mats set for lunch, we settled ourselves in the sunshine which brightened our dining area. I listened as Bob told me how he had waited at the escrow office observing the difficulty the secretary had in finding a place to put telephone messages so they would not be overlooked. She wrote each phone message on a little pink "While You Were Out" slip, and then searched for a place to put it. She propped some at strategic spots near a phone or on a stack of papers, tucked some under corners of desk mats, and finally put one, evidently an important one, on the seat of her boss's swivel chair where it couldn't be ignored.

While he watched, Bob visualized a solution, and that is what he enthusiastically explained to me as he drew a cross section of a product that launched us into a new business and new adventures.

The product was the Call-Back Message Holder. The business: R&D Products, Inc. When Bob died in 1999, he had fifteen patents. A sixteenth one was issued posthumously. R&D Products is now owned by our son, Tom, and his wife, Robyn.

"Why doesn't somebody figure a way to fix that?" or, after the fact, "That's so simple, why didn't I think of it?" Bob's talent: finding simple solutions to real problems. With the aid of a yellow ruled pad clasped to a crummy clipboard, he created a life of independence and left a legacy of integrity, creativity, and love.

♄

Linda Hawrus, Erik Luckas, Ted Young, Joanne Danenhower, Joanna Deeley, Robyn, Dorothy, John, Bob and Tom Hansen, circa 1993

THE BIRTH OF THE CALL-BACK MESSAGE HOLDER

Bob's idea for a discrete place to put telephone messages was so exciting to me I told him, "Forget the tumble box." A prototype-in-process of the tumble box was Bob's current project. The tumble box was Bob's idea for a small composter, suitable for use in urban areas, where living in an apartment would not preclude one from recycling food wastes. It was a good idea but another inventor later patented and marketed a composter very similar to Bob's design. We had no regrets. For us, the Call-Back offered the greater potential.

On his yellow pad Bob sketched a three dimensional view and a cross section of the product. The idea was to fit a plastic holder into the cavity beneath the cradle of a standard desk phone. The upright portion of the holder had a cut-out finger (or tongue) to hold messages where they couldn't be missed. There they were, in unobstructed view, right on the phone itself.

Think of all the phones, of all the secretaries, of all the messages!

Whoa. Not so fast. The gleam in the inventor's eye to the conception and birth of a viable commercial product is just the beginning. Like having a kid, the hard work begins at first sight. The gleam came in the spring of 1973. The first Call-Back was sold three years later, in the spring of 1976.

When I saw Bob sitting with his head back, held by interlocking fingers, with a vacuous look on his face, I knew he was working on the Call-Back design. There would soon be a sketch on the yellow pad, and then a time to talk about it.

The design evolved over a period of months, then the quest for the best plastic to use began.

Bob's research was thorough. The plastic needed to be sturdy, yet flexible. The cut-out finger (or tongue) needed a memory...that is, it would return to its normal position whether it held one, a few, or many messages. In addition, it had to be pleasing to the eye. Acrylic was ruled out quickly. Its tendency to crack made it unacceptable even though it was attractive and cheap. Soon, catalogs from plastic manufacturers filled our mailbox. Bob ordered samples. He purchased items in local stores that were made of plastic that might meet our requirements. We were learning from scratch and the success of the product depended on the plastic we chose, so this was a basic decision to make. The winner? Polycarbonate...so tough motorcycle helmets are made from it, so flexible the tongue could be bent ninety degrees, and with a memory like an elephant. For the broadest acceptance, we chose to make the message holder, in clear polycarbonate, and that presented a problem.

The clearer the polycarbonate, the costlier it was.

The choice to have the message holder produced in crystal clear polycarbonate laid the foundation for our marketing policy. Before we had a name for it, we knew we would offer only the best quality product.

On our twenty-fifth wedding anniversary, son Tom gave us twenty-five silver dollars. Having dinner out was a treat for us, so we used his gift for a romantic dinner at the vine-covered Vineyards Inn on Calistoga Road east of Santa Rosa. Then, in November, 1973, twenty-five dollars bought two delicious entrees including wine, dessert and tip. We had barely given our order to the waiter than we started talking about a name for the message holder. Whether it was the wine or the ambiance, we thought we had a winner with...oh dear, I hate to tell you...CALL-BACK RACK.

It was weeks later when the corniness of it embarrassed us. Call-Back Rack, Call-Back Rack. Call-Back Rack. No, not that. One friend who was in on the beginning of our venture called it by that name until she died.

With something to call it by and a sheet of polycarbonate, Bob set about to make a prototype of his idea. He designed a wooden jig to make the model. He fitted the polycarbonate into the jig, heated it in kitchen oven at a low temperature. Under Bob's watchful eye, the plastic warmed and when molded to the desired shape, Bob took it out to cool. Quietly we waited. When Bob thought it was cool enough, he carefully removed it from the mold, and it was perfect!

The learning curve was getting steeper. Patenting? Getting a commercial mold made? New challenges lay ahead.

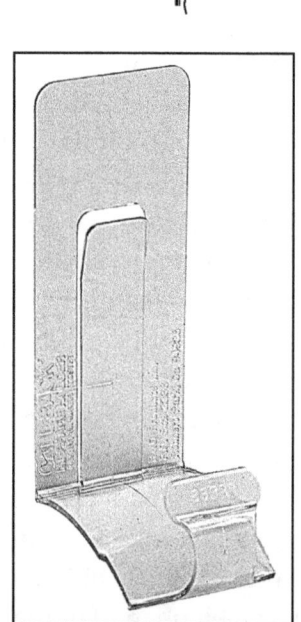

176, Call Back message holder

EYE OF A NEEDLE

"...easier for camels to get through needles' eyes than
for rich people to get into the kingdom of heaven...."
The Needle's Eye, Margaret Drabble

In British author Margaret Drabble's 1972 novel, The Needle's Eye, her protagonist, young heiress Rose Vassiliou, sick of her parents' preoccupation with money and materialism, vowed that she would never possess anything that she feared to lose. "It was a very solemn vow...I went upstairs and made myself a special prayer to God...and then I went out into the garden and vowed, under a tree that I thought was specially sacred. And that was that." When Rose was twenty-four, she received a sizeable inheritance and promptly wrote a check for almost all of it to Akisoferi Nyoka—"...her hand trembling, her heart beating loudly in her frightened chest, exhilarated beyond bearing by the extremity, the irrevocability of the act, by its irreversible determining quality, by its implications, by its very size"—to pay for a school in Central Africa.

Reading the novel one day last week, I was reminded of a diminished version of Rose's story in my own life. Bob, and I lived in Doylestown, Pennsylvania, about twenty-five miles north of Philadelphia, for almost four years—from the beginning of 1979 to the fall of 1982. As newcomers we looked for opportunities to participate in community life and soon associated ourselves with a group opposed to nuclear power. It called itself The Clean Energy Collective, and it was a lively group, most of its members being in their twenties and thirties while we were in our sixties.

The regional power company proposed building a nuclear power plant on the Delaware River in a location much too close to the heavily populated Philadelphia area. The Collective, besides organizing the opposition with educational meetings and picket lines, put its energies into study and research to prepare to testify at hearings held by the Nuclear Regulatory Commission.

One outstanding researcher in the Collective, Phyllis Zitzer, was a young woman who prepared her presentations before the NRC so well she outshone the professional expert witnesses. There was an urgency to her studies as the utility company was moving quickly to get approval to build Limerick (the name they gave the proposed plant). Adding pressure to the work to be done, the accident at the nuclear power plant at Three Mile Island near Harrisburg exploded the fear of those living downwind from that plant. Phyllis gave up her job and worked full time for the cause, living on the good will of her landlord and the contributions of friends and family. She did not live well, and the clunker she drove was testimony to her poverty and devotion. Bob and I admired Phyllis. She was a high school graduate and had an ordinary kind of office job. Her interest in nuclear power came about because she lived on the Perkiomen River, one of the water resources for the proposed Limerick power plant. When we returned to California in late 1982, Phyllis was spending a good part of her time at the State Capitol continuing her research and appearances at hearings.

About eight years later, Bob and I found time to visit some of our Doylestown friends when we attended a trade show in Philadelphia. We asked Mary Ellen Noble, one of the activists in The Clean Energy Collective, about Phyllis. "Is she still driving that old car?" Mary Ellen nodded her head, "Yes, but I don't see how she does it. It's past being on its last leg." She told us Phyllis was just as earnest as ever—never a whimper about her chosen state of poverty to pursue what she thought she needed to do, and never a sign of burn out.

As Bob and I had dinner, we sat silently, absorbed in thought. Finally, either I or Bob said, "Are you thinking what I'm thinking?" And he or I responded, "I think so." We looked at each other and smiled. "Let's do it," we said.

The next morning, we checked with the Nissan dealer and picked up some color brochures on the latest model station wagons. A call to our credit union in Rohnert Park, California, assured us we could make an auto loan. We called Phyllis and arranged an early evening meeting at her place. On our arrival, we saw her dilapidated car in the driveway and knew we were doing the right thing. Our first glimpse of her apartment startled us. It was a work place filled with brick and plank shelving holding masses of files and papers...all neat and retrievable. Hers was obviously a singularly focused life.

After exchanging warm greetings, we handed her the brochures from the car dealer saying she should choose the color she wanted. The "I can't believe this is happening" expression on her face when she hesitantly but fully understood what we meant was our sufficient reward: the high that comes with a "random act of kindness" lasts a long, happy time.

Bob and I paid for the insurance while the title for the station wagon was in our name. For four years we made monthly payments to the credit union. We sometimes groaned when yet another parking ticket or invoices from a fender bender arrived in our mail while Phyllis focused on her task opposing nuclear power. But time passed, the loan was paid off, we sent her the pink slip, and life moved on. We've lost touch, but now, fifteen years later, it's a safe bet that she still has the wagon and is still skillfully, involved in some worthy cause.

And what happened with Rose Vassiliou's act of kindness? Mr. Nyoka bought himself a big white Cadillac, the school was built and used for a few months before it was burned to the ground during a tribal war. Neither Rose nor Bob or I had any regrets.

12 W

The story goes that President Kennedy, when traveling with Ted Sorenson and other members of his staff on Air Force One or in a chauffeur-driven automobile, passed the time by playing a favorite word game: one person chose an answer and the others provided the appropriate question. In an example that I once read, the answer given was "9 W" and the question was "Do you spell your name with a V, Dr. Wagner?" "Nein, W."

My story is about my sister Pat's feet. She wore a size 12 W shoe. A less free spirit could not have endured the clumsy clodhoppers she wore.

Pat was born in 1910, long before shoe manufacturers acknowledged the need to make shoes that fit women of all foot sizes. With closets full of ill-fitting, unwearable shoes, and hundreds, perhaps thousands, of dollars ill-spent in the search for an attractive size 12 W, Pat forced her feet into whatever she could get, even pointy-toed disasters when they were the fashion of the day. Pat's only real choice, no matter where she shopped, was the color of the plain, laced oxford that was her burden to bear... a burden she bore with good cheer. However, it's hard to be coquettish in a size 12 shoe.

Pat, circa 1986

Visiting in California in the early 1970s, Pat walked into a Berkeley shoe store and looked wistfully at the fancy, dainty shoes on display. The courteous clerk asked how he could help her. "What style of shoe do you have in mind?" "Just something for streetwalking," she said.

By the time the clerk noted she had only one eye, a 60-year-old largish body dressed in a proper cotton Schroeder classic shirtwaist, with those big feet in Godawful shoes, she realized what she had said and started laughing. Pat's laugh rippling out from her rib cage put the clerk at ease and they had a great time with Pat getting to know about him and his family and how come he was a shoe clerk and did he know her sister-in-law—and with the clerk selling her shoes right and left.

Pat lived in Bartlesville, Oklahoma, in a big, old, beautiful, airplane bungalow style home with a porch all across the front of the house. In the summertime, a screen door served as the only barrier between a visitor and the inhabitants. One morning Pat, barefoot and dressed in a cotton sun dress anticipating a hot day, answered the doorbell to be greeted by a tall, cheerful looking middle-aged man. He was a door-to-door salesman who found it easy to strike up a conversation with Pat. They continued talking long after Pat made it clear to him she was not interested in whatever it was he was selling.

Pat's quick smile

After a while, he said, "M'am, do you mind telling me what size shoe you wear?" Pat laughed. "Why, no," she said. "I wear a size 12 wide." "Can I ask you a favor? Would you mind opening the screen door so I can take a look at your feet?" Pat obligingly opened the screen door. He gawked at her feet, and before turning around to leave, he shook his head saying, "Thank you, ma'am. My wife will never believe this!"

If it's true that people who need people are the luckiest people in the world, Pat was a winner. Wearing size 12W shoes, my one-eyed sister Pat laughed, and her world laughed with her.

THE SIX-LEGGED COW

How can you express yourself when you are totally frustrated? What can you say when you feel put-upon, used, dominated, diminished? Once when I worked in a large commercial office I was at the copying center when a young secretary came fuming into the room. She slammed down the papers she had brought to copy and sputtered, "I wish I didn't say f---k all the time. Now I don't have a word to use when I really need it!"

In 1951 when Bob and I lived in an apartment in Mrs. Barnett's house on Manhattan Beach Boulevard in Manhattan Beach, California, there was a small ranch across the street from us. On that ranch there was a six-legged cow. At an angle of about fifteen or twenty degrees midway on its hind legs another set of legs protruded. Although the cow did not seem discomforted by this unusual arrangement of body parts, it was an oddity. Passersby stopped to gawk and it was one of the first things we showed my young nephew when he came from Oklahoma to visit us that summer. Bill looked at the cow with curiosity, but he seemed to have an empathy for her, sensing that she would like to have four legs like the others and frustrated that she could do nothing about it.

Pat and her husband Howard and three of their children, fourteen-year-old Susan, and ten year olds David and Bill, had driven from Oklahoma to see us. They wanted the kids to experience the ocean, to play on the beach, and especially to take Susan to Hollywood. Susan was a super fan of Roy Rogers. They had tickets for a show where Roy and his wife and horse would appear in person. Susan was beside herself with excitement when the day came for them to go. Not so with Bill.

Bill was active. He was not one to be confined for even a short period, and he did not want to sit in that car another minute. The long ride from Oklahoma was more than enough for him and he was sick to death sitting in the back seat with Susan listening to her drool about Roy Rogers.

Both Bob and I had to go to work so he couldn't stay with us: he was stuck with another day cooped up in a car. Even worse, he had to get dressed up. Dressed up meant he had to wear shoes and put on a shirt with buttons.

On the day of their trip to Hollywood, when I walked out with Pat and Howard and Susan to the car, I saw Bill slouched in the back seat, looking kind of cute in his nice clean clothes and his hair all combed. But I never saw such a sour face. He was glum, his face contorted with grimaces.

"What in the world is the matter with you?" I asked. He screwed up his face and, as his misery overflowed, he sputtered, "I feel just like a six-legged cow!"

Now, whenever I get that six-legged cow feeling, I am soon out of my misery just thinking of Bill and his car ride to Hollywood that summer day long ago.

♄

David, Howard, Dorothy, Bill, Pat and Susan, circa 1951

PRESERVING THE LEGACY

About two months after Bob died, he received a letter from Paradigm Productions, Inc., in Berkeley, California, asking for personal home movies, high quality photographs, letters and newspaper articles to be used in making a documentary film. The documentary, The Good War and Those Who Refused to Fight It, focused on individuals like Bob, a former Civilian Public Service member, who "refused to fight in World War II for moral and religious reasons, exploring the pacifist traditions you inherited, the moral dilemmas you faced, the families who supported or rejected your choice, and the C.O.s (conscientious objectors) impact on medical, social and cultural reforms in the post World War II years."

I did not respond to Paradigm's letter dated April 10, 1999. I found it the other night when I was going through old papers in a fruitless search for the pink slip on my automobile.

The letter was in its envelope addressed on the outside to HANSEN, ROBERT S. and on the inside to "Dear former Civilian Public Service member". It caught my interest for I had chanced to see the film the letter proposed, "The Good War and Those Who Refused to Fight It," on public TV a few nights earlier. Did the finished product match their good intentions even though there was no input from Bob's viewpoint or from me as his widow?

Bob and I met in Detroit in 1948. We were married in November of that year. In the few months of our courtship and the fifty years of our marriage, I heard many stories of his days and years as a conscientious objector. Although his stories didn't make it into this film, I am glad that it was made.

THE CARD

In 1947, the Christmas card I received from my family in Oklahoma was the same card I had sent them the year before! On it Mother had written, "You didn't think this would kick back to you, did you, Dodo?"

The Card has been kicking around every year since. For 20 years it traveled cross country. Since Mother's death, we display The Card each year as a treasured part of our holiday traditions.

Mother's little verse on The Card she sent in 1958 carries my wish for you:

This card has traveled, oh, so many miles
And brought to me so many smiles,
I hope this year that it will do
The very same thing from me to you!

PART THREE: MY LATER YEARS

AN INTERVIEW WITH ME AT 84

Diana Rodriguez is a sophomore at Boston University and one of five students sharing a dorm suite with my granddaughter, Clare Hansen. In a recent late night phone call, Clare asked me if I would be willing to be interviewed by Diana for a paper she needed for one of her classes.

Diana's class is called "Health and Disability Across the Lifespan" and the purpose of the paper is "to contrast the way older people live today to the way they lived life in the past." Of course I agreed.

Q. Tell me a little about yourself. What is a typical day for you?

A. For an elderly person, I consider myself lucky. Sitting down and getting up are more embarrassing than painful; I occasionally use a cane when I'm climbing the block-long hill from downtown; and I run out of steam as I neaten up before company comes, but it doesn't seem to matter as good friends don't care if the house isn't sparkling.

Dorothy, circa 2004

Other than that, I think I do pretty well for someone who's less than a couple of months from 85. I prepare my own meals, clean house, do the laundry, and the grocery shopping. I hate to drive, but I can walk the few blocks to the library, senior center, pharmacy, post office and hair salon. I could walk to Safeway but I'd rather support local businesses, so I drive to Fircrest Market, a locally owned business that's in Sebastopol where I live. My doctor is close enough for me to drive there, but I call on my sons or friends for more distant outings.

Although I love being with people, I find I'm not lonely living by myself. I value the sacred silence at my Quaker meeting and the public silence of standing with Women in Black mourning all victims of violence. My husband Bob died almost six years ago: living with him for fifty years prepared me for living without him. Being involved in the world, letting go, loving unconditionally, having fun— all are things I do better because of him.

A typical day? For me, that's an oxymoron. I guess a typical day for me is spending a ridiculous amount of time looking for things I have used within the past ten minutes, wasting endless hours trying to do something urgent that my computer forbids me to do; and wondering why in the world I am so slow in getting things accomplished.

Other than that I tend my little patio garden; pay attention to Jackson, my faithful feline companion; lose at Scrabble; write stories for my Life History Writing Class; attend LHWC once a week; cook stuff for potlucks; have long phone conversations with my four remaining siblings; keep up on politics; do personal and household chores; host a weekly group knitting warm things for Afghanistan refugees; have lunch with friends; listen to KPFA, free speech radio; check e-mails for latest progressive news (Truthout, Commondreams, Moveon) and for longed-for messages from family and friends. My typical day is guided by my mantra: For things to change, I must change.

Q. What are some of your favorite activities? Least favorite?
A. Favorite:
- Relishing time with family, personal friends, and with people I know in groups—my writing class, Sauerkraut Sorority, book group, Quakers, Women in Black, and Taxes for Peace friends.
- Writing memoirs and other stories
- Participation in socially conscious organizations
- Reading - Fiction: novels, short stories Non-fiction: biographies, current affairs

Least favorite:
- Driving
- Shopping in malls

Q. Looking back at your life, what are two of your favorite memories?
A. Only two? These were life changing:

1. In the mid-1940s, I answered an ad in a Washington, D.C. newspaper, for employment at Rochdale Consumers Cooperative, Inc. My interview lasted several hours as Robert Volkhausen, the interviewer, answered my question, "What is a consumer cooperative? When he told me the democratic principles of businesses owned and controlled by the people who use them, I knew that was the practical application of the concept of the "brotherhood of man" philosophy I strongly embraced . I liked the idea of businesses run for service, not for profit, and could envision how that could affect relationships in every aspect of society...even eliminating the motivation for war. I got the job, and from then on co-ops were my passion and my "religion."

2. In May of 1948, I stood in the aisle near the soup display at the new Motor City Co-op Market on Warren Avenue in Detroit when I overheard a tall young man telling a customer how the co-op differed from an ordinary store. I was impressed by his knowledge of co-ops. so when the customer had moved on, I approached him. Part of my job as Education Secretary of the co-op was to seek people to participate, so I asked if he'd like to serve on a committee. He would and

did. That young man, Bob Hansen, who had just arrived as a new employee, became my husband six months later. We fell in love in front of the soups at Motor City Co-op...and lived happily ever after.

Q. What are two things you would like to accomplish right now or in the near future?

A. 1. I hope to improve my writing skills so family members will want to read the memoirs I write...memoirs to help them value the heritage and family culture that is part of who they are.

2. I am a pacifist. I believe it is wrong for me to kill a person, or to pay for someone to be killed. Therefore, I am a war tax resister. I want to bring this opportunity, its benefits and risks, to the consciousness of like-minded citizens. I am working with our local Taxes for Peace group to support a national peace tax fund and, through workshops and publicity, to encourage opposition to paying taxes for war—even if it's only a letter sent in with the tax return. My aim is to improve my knowledge and skills to be more effective in peacemaking.

Q. Tell me about your friends and family members.

A. Sadly, I have fewer now than I did at the beginning of the year. Nine close friends and family members have died in 2004. Of the original nine children born to my parents, there are five of us left. My oldest brother is 96, another is 74, and the youngest is 72. My remaining sister is 76. There are 100 people in my family: 66 of them attended the memorial service for my oldest sister, Pat, who died in January at age 94. The newest member, a great-niece, was born on November 29th.

I have spoken of friends in other parts of this interview. The depth and diversity of my friendships brings me much comfort and pleasure.

Q. Do you participate in some sort of physical activity each week? What kinds?

A. I try, but am not very consistent. My goal is a minimum of six hours of walking a week. It's probably closer to three. On days I don't walk, I do at least a half hour of exercise to start the day...leg lifts, arm twirls, next twists, deep breathing, etc. If by chance I do both in one day I feel pretty proud of myself.

Q. How important is physical health in your well-being and quality of life today?

A. I really don't think about it all the time, so I guess it's not my top priority. Arthritis bothers me some, but nothing like the pain and deformity suffered by my mother and two of my sisters. I feel pretty healthy without being obsessed about longevity.

Q. Would you consider yourself to have a disability of any sort? If so, how does it affect your life right now?

A. Yes. At my regular checkup yesterday, my lab work showed a sharp rise in blood glucose count. I have had non-insulin dependent diabetes for a number of years. I take oral medications for the diabetes. A major heart attack in February 1995, remains vivid in my memory, sufficient that I carry a supply of nitroquick with me at all times—just in case.

Q. What is one message you would give to my generation, if you could say anything?

A. Be smart enough and kind enough to figure out—and implement—ways for us to live on this planet without killing each other.

Q. What other sorts of things are important to you right now that I may not have asked?

A. You've covered a lot. Thanks for asking me to be interviewed. It's been thought-provoking and made me realize how grateful I am for the women before me who struggled for the rights and opportunities I now enjoy.

♮

VISIONS

September 17, 2001.

Like the characters in the Ann Tyler novel I was reading, I'd had an ordinary sort of day filled with routine chores and choices. I stayed up past my bedtime to finish her soul-satisfying story, snuggled under the covers, and closed my eyes when I had the unsettling feeling that things were moving in the room. Cloudlike things, clusters of dishwater colored strings and curlicues, big as a bread box. When I opened my eyes, same thing, only more distinct. I looked directly at the bedside light: it disintegrated into cloudy gaseous puffs and bubbles. The ceiling light fixture, picture frames, anything of material substance became nebulous. All was in motion—a mass of dull gray mystical shapes swirling and twisting. The upper two or three feet of my bedroom was a scene of wild commotion.

Surprisingly, I felt no fear. No panic. I was not woozy or nauseated. I was a calm, interested observer of uncommon confusion around me. What could cause this to happen?

My room is not pitch dark at night, even with the Venetian blinds closed. There's light and shadow from the moon and the trees and the wind. Light from a digital clock and various small electrical and electronic devices normally gives the room a slightly rosy hue. Deliberately, I looked for a possible cause of the phenomenon but found nothing to account for what I saw.

I sat up and put some artificial tears in my eyes thinking that might clear my vision—and my mind. I lay down facing the wall and closed my eyes with the hope I could ignore the turmoil around me.

Instead, even with my eyes closed and covered with my hand, wildly moving objects—entirely different from the ones in the rest of the room—covered the wall as if the wall were a screen upon which a live movie was in progress. Precisely rectangular, smaller and even more active than the nebulae below the ceiling, the wild things gyrated upward with a dizzying speed. In one spot there were multiple rectangles with dots in rows, reminding me of peg boards without pegs. In another area, slightly above and to the left, I saw tiny, shiny black tubes, zillions of them, rapidly revolving in utter disarray. To the right was an area in a rosy sepia tone with hundreds of cluttered rectangular shapes submerged in thousands of blank post-it notes flying around as in a New York ticker tape parade. With my eyes opened or closed, I saw the same "visions" in the same places no matter if several minutes elapsed between glances. The only bright color was a metallic blue object, shaped like a little VW bug, scooting around on a cloudy cushion on my chest.

Fascinated as I was by the surreal assemblage around me, I wondered, is this how it feels to go blind? Is this what happens when a retina detaches? I knew it was not a nightmare: I was awake and alert to my surroundings. Or, had my absorption in the tragedy of the terrorist attack on the World Trade Center on September 11th, viewing the TV images again and again and again, addled my vision...or my brain?

Finally, I fell asleep reminding myself to remember what I had experienced — and to call my doctor first thing in the morning.

♄

OUR FIRST GRANDCHILD IS BORN

When Karen, my first daughter-in-law, was awaiting the birth of our first grandchild, it was her habit and my pleasure for her to stop in and visit me. She and John lived near Julliard Park in Santa Rosa, Bob and I lived on Glenwood Court near Sonoma Avenue, so it was an easy ride to get on her bike and come over.

Joel with grandmother Dorothy, circa 1976

Karen was tall, twenty years old, and pretty with her long blonde hair (parted in the center, in the plain way hippie girls wore their hair in 1976). She liked being a mother-to-be and it showed. I wondered if the people along her route took note of her changing appearance as the pregnancy progressed. If they did, they might have ventured a guess as to how soon and how big, for she carried her bigness in a forthright manner, and big she was.

It was no surprise to Bob and me when John let us know late on an April afternoon that he had taken Karen to nearby Memorial Hospital. We weren't nervous as Karen was strong and healthy and it was obvious she was ready. However, as the evening wore on and we didn't hear from him, we had the idea of going to the hospital. No, we thought, remembering the birth of John, our first born, this is their time. I don't remember whether I slept soundly or had dreams of becoming a grandmother. I do remember awakening with a concern that we hadn't heard from John. Again, remembering his birth, he took his own sweet time, be patient, I told Bob. It was a message meant for me. The morning wore on. Then there was a little knock on the front door. It couldn't be John. Maybe a neighbor. My mind was busy as I took the few steps from the kitchen to the door to open it.

It was Karen. On her bicycle. Baby still inside. I welcomed her in and we shared stories about contractions that never went anywhere and the disappointment of being sent home without a baby. Was it a day or days later when, on April 10, 1976, Joel Curtis Hansen arrived in good shape? No newborn prune face on him! At 11 pounds 4 ounces, he was wrinkle free and beautiful to behold, well worth the wait.

♄

Chris and Joel with grandmother Dorothy at Alicia's High School Graduation, circa 2002

MY FAVORITE LAST GRANDDAUGHTER

Dorothy, Clare and Ann

Grandmas have a reputation for being worry warts. I include myself in that category as my own behavior bolsters the stereotype of the anxious grandma fretting about the future. Especially, I worried about my granddaughter Ann even before she was born. I believed she would have a hard life. She wouldn't have a chance, I thought. And nothing could be done about it. Facts are facts. She would always and forever be the little sister of fabulous Clare, now two years old, my favorite first granddaughter.

Ann Louise Hansen was born in Eugene, Oregon, on September 30, 1987, into a family of high achievers. Her mother, Sonja, a dietician, had completed her master's degree, and her father, my son Paul, a physical therapist, was working on his doctorate at the University of Oregon. Test results for precocious Clare ranked her as a genius.

Why wouldn't I worry? Ann spent her babyhood with her left thumb in her mouth and her right hand clinging to whatever part of her mother or her mother's garments was closest. She really liked elbows.

I wish my mother had lived to know Ann. She would have loved her. Who wouldn't? Who didn't? She was adorable. Ann's lovability was not the point. The question was: how could she stand in her own light when she was stuck smack-dab in Clare's shadow?

Worrying is permissible: meddling is not. I tried to keep my concerns to myself. Although we kept in close touch by letter and phone, Bob and I were absentee grandparents to our granddaughters.

Holiday and vacation visits had to suffice as their family moved from Oregon to Wisconsin to Flagstaff, Arizona, where we visited them at Easter time in 1990. Our welcome was hardly what we expected. Not only was it freezing cold with snow on the ground, but when we were greeted at the door by Sonja, there were no granddaughters flying into our arms with a show of unbounded joy in our arrival.

As I looked around for them, I finally spotted Clare curled up on a stair-step with her head pulled into her shoulders uttering a tiny chirpy squeal every few seconds, completely ignoring us. I looked behind Sonja to find Ann sucking her favorite thumb and kneading her mother's elbow. After a spell, the girls cozied up to us on the sofa. That is, Ann did, thumb in mouth, as she warmed up to Bob. Clare wormed her way down the stairs, snuck across the room on all fours, silently squiggled onto the sofa with her soft mouse body curled next to me and her little paws and whiskers brushing against my face. It was a full five minutes that she lay snuggled against me before she transformed herself from mouse to my loving granddaughter.

Among Ann's gifts on Easter day were two little-girl purses, one from her other grandma and the other from her Uncle Tom and Aunt Robyn. The purses were very different in appearance but each was appropriate for the sweet shy girl that was Ann. No sooner had the gifts been unwrapped than Clare began her assault: she was determined to have one of those purses. She worked on Ann.

Clare (sweetly): I didn't get a purse. Could I have one of yours? Please.
Ann: No.
Clare: (cloyingly): Could we play together with them?
Ann: No.
Clare (more so): Could I play with the pink one...for just a little while?
Ann: No.
Later.
Clare (whining): Mom, Ann has two purses. I don't have any. That's not fair.
Clare (angry): Ann, you're not fair. You should share.
Ann: No..

Clare's sweet talk, coaxing, pleading, chicanery, all failed. Ann stayed calmly resolute. At bedtime, she still had her two purses. Coming down for breakfast, she held one in each hand.

It was then that I stopped worrying about Ann.

When Ann was still a preschooler, Sonja, Ann and I were shopping in a department store. I spotted a dress which I thought would be perfect for Ann, and was prepared to buy it for her. I called her over. "Ann, come look. Isn't this cute?" She took a quick look, shrugged and said, "It's not my style."

She's followed her own unique style right through to this, her freshman year at the University of Washington in Seattle. I won't list her many accomplishments for fear of bragging (another reputation grandmothers happily earn)—I'll just mention a few: she's an accomplished violinist, expert volleyball player, fine scholar...and I'll tell you one little story so you'll know how she shines in her own light.

Ann graduated from Wilson High School in Tacoma, Washington, last June 13th. Her mother's birthday was on June 12. Somehow, in the midst of celebrating this big event in her own life (the prom, the parties, the good-byes, the honors, the graduation ceremony), Ann—with the help of her boyfriend Andrew—planned a surprise party for the big event in her mother's life; it was Sonja's fiftieth birthday. I was there and I was proud.

For all my worry, Ann is not intimidated by her sister Clare. They are the best of friends. And she is positively my very favorite last granddaughter.

♭

DEAR ALICIA

Dear Alicia,

Your twenty-first birthday seems a fine time for me to tell you how special you are in my life. From the very day you were born, we've had close ties. I was there at Community Hospital on May 4, 1984, with your mom. Although I didn't go into the delivery room with her and the doctor, I was watching through the clear glass windows as you came into this world. You were healthy and pretty from the very start! Lucky you—to be welcomed with such love by your mom and Joel and Chris, and your grandpa and so many more, including Bob and me.

I have pictures to prove that you've been a strong, independent female from early on. There's that Christmas photograph with Joel and Chris taken when you were just a preschooler where you look mad enough to take on the world! It's hard to believe that same child grew up to be the confident, glamorous gal in your high school graduation photos. I can believe it because I've been around to watch you develop and to be proud of every big step you've taken.

Alicia Moss, circa 2002

You know already how much I admire your strength of character: to make the right choices and to make changes as new challenges occur. I like the way you give of yourself so openhandedly, your ability to express your love and affection and your concern for others, even those whose lives and circumstances are far removed from your own. Your choice of study in environmental sciences is just one example of your generous nature...you're not a me-firster.

A good student, a loyal friend, a reliable employee, a happy camper. You're all of those, but how come you are those AND a wild adventurer? Where do you get the energy, the stamina, the determination to jump out of airplanes and run the NIKE 26-mile race? I stand in awe of you, my young dear friend, and wish you the best on this day and the rest of your life.

Much love from your not quite a grandma.

NEW DIMENSIONS

On our fiftieth wedding anniversary on November 5, 1998, Bob was in a wheelchair, gravely ill, partially paralyzed by painful Guillan Barre Syndrome. Bob died on February 21, 1999. In the years since his death, I have learned to live alone. Whatever sense of serenity and success I have attained, I credit in large measure to my fifty years with Bob. Yesterday, I was privileged to spend some time in quiet reflection of this good man's life.

If Bob were still alive we would have celebrated his 86th birthday yesterday in our usual low-key manner. Our sons sometimes kidded us saying a walk to the library was our idea of a celebration. That's not so. We had our traditions...special gatherings with favorite people, food and rituals...but Bob and I were consummately contented. We didn't need a big show to feel honored and loved.

Rainbow outside dining room window 2-21-99

On the morning of Bob's death in 1999 a spectacular, luminous triple-rainbow enlivened the February sky. It caught the attention of Bob's mourning family with its brightness and dominance. Its significance in its beauty, timeliness, and even its location — for it could not have been seen from any other part of the house—seemed beyond the ordinary, explainable phenomenon of the reflection and refraction of the sun's rays upon drops of rain that makes a rainbow. Some might say this was the moment that Bob's soul entered Heaven, but that seemed an inappropriate assumption for a family such as ours. It was only a month or so before his death that Bob, when listening to some beautiful music, confessed that he was "not 1000% agnostic."

Although Bob and I were active members of protestant churches — he, Lutheran, and I, Methodist — in our childhood and teens, we weaned ourselves away from church in our twenties. He was more interested in good works than in pious musings: he served as a conscientious objector in World War II and worked as an employee or volunteer in consumer-owned cooperatives most of his life. A loving, liberal family, we were not churchgoers, nor much inclined toward conversation about religion or spirituality. As for myself, I expected to live my life without Bob in a practical, healthful way, confident of the caring support of family and friends. I was not prepared for mystical events entering my life. Was I in for a surprise?

When Bob died he was 78 years old. Consistent with his wishes we donated his body to the University of California Medical School in San Francisco. On the following Wednesday, Patsy (my son John's love) came by for lunch. A phone call for Patsy interrupted our meal, and while she was away from the table, the view outside the dining room window demanded my attention.

There, filling the sky, occupying the space held by the vanished rainbow, framed by soft white clouds, was Bob. The color photo on the front of Bob's memorial program that son Tom had created for me magically enlarged to celestial size. For just a moment, wearing his brown winter hat, plaid shirt and knitted sweater, Bob smiled down at me. The vision, if that's what to call it, vanished before Patsy returned to the table.

Bob's photo from memorial program

What did it mean? Was I hallucinating from grief? Would that image have been there if I were sitting on the opposite side of the table? Why in the sky? I have never envisaged Heaven above nor Hell below. The sky has held no more meaning for me than wind or rain or acts of kindness as reservoirs of the soul. I had no answers, but I felt an inexplicable comfort.

A few months later, Bob came to me when I was visiting at my brother's home in Florida. A vision so distinct, so tangible, it is still real to me.

No wheelchair, no sign of paralysis or pain, Bob showed no evidence of the Guillain Barré syndrome that caused his death. On a balmy spring day Bob drove a flashy convertible (our car was an older Maxima) across a winding California road, vaguely like Sonoma County's Coleman Valley Road, toward the ocean. Easy, relaxing. We watched the newborn lambs wobble to their moms' teats, marveled as the white-tailed kite hovered precisely over his prey below, and covered our ears as the gulls squawked among themselves as they flew overhead. And then Bob was gone. Next morning at breakfast, I related my story to Jack and Linda, my brother and his wife. I thought if I told it, the story would cease to feel so real, but it never came down to dream-size.

My experiences of seeing Bob's face in the sky and of taking that lovely ride with him occurred shortly after his death, and I assumed they were a necessary part of the enormity of my grief at that time.

I met Shirley in the bereavement support group I attended. Ken, her husband of sixty years, died about a month after Bob's death. There were angels on her shoulders that helped her communicate with Ken. My tolerance for varying manifestations of grief broadened as we shared our stories in the group. I learned to appreciate Shirley's clairvoyance. She was the first to know of my next meeting with Bob.

More than a year passed before Bob came to me again. This time, in the middle of the night, in an ethereal setting reminiscent of Kahlil Gibran's illustrations in The Prophet, Bob was dressed in a flowing garment of white. I clung to him but as I felt myself reluctantly floating earthward from his embrace, Bob gently told me "Go home. Go home." When my tears dried and I reflected on my vision, I interpreted Bob's message to mean that I should live out my life as my own, not as his widow. Shirley confirmed my interpretation. I believed I had seen my last vision of Bob.

Soon, I moved from the home we had shared into a little apartment on Wilton Avenue in Sebastopol. Bob knows where it is.

A few months ago Bob came calling. In the middle of the night, I was awakened by a very small sound. I sat up in bed and listened carefully. The front door opened. Through the darkness, through the walls, I could see Bob as he entered. Standing straight and tall, wearing his droopy blue cotton hat, with an armload of books from the library, he was real enough to touch. But I was too slow: he was gone before I could get out of bed.

I felt good about Bob's visit. Some weeks later I shared my experience with my next door neighbor, Carol. As I told the story, her eyes widened with interest. She could scarcely wait until I stopped talking to exclaim, "You won't believe this." Michael, her grown son who lives in Marin County and stays over with her occasionally asked her, "Who was that tall man I saw going into Dorothy's apartment last night?"

"What did he look like?"

"I saw only the back of him. He had on a light colored hat. That's all I know."

Not a nosey neighbor, Carol had not mentioned Michael's observations to me. Now she and I realized that my vision and Michael's sighting were on the same night!

It's been ten years since Bob died. These visits from him have added welcome new dimensions to my life. When I die I don't expect to see Bob or the Pearly Gates, but if I do, I will just say, "I wasn't 1000% agnostic."

♄

The skinny tall tree from Jack and Mattie

AN HOUR OF SUNSHINE

After a week of stormy weather, this new day broke with the promise of change. I was ready for it, with a soul that needed nourishment and a loaded laundry basket. Clear blue skies peeked through the dark clouds and waited for them to release a modest downpour of rain before reappearing for a tentative claim on the future. I hoped to do several loads of laundry, making a run for the laundry room during the blue-skies period.

I had to wait for the dryer to finish so I could put a new load in. I thought it would be only a minute or two, so I stepped outside with the fresh air all around, and wondered if I should get the little pruners and a paper bag to put the prunees in...it will take just a second to get them from a cupboard in the kitchen, and I can stop when the dryer goes off.

I started clipping off water-soaked, dead roses and snapdragons and strawberry leaves. And cutting dead grasses. And trimming back the honeysuckle, and the mock orange, and the red lipstick plant. And I was thinking I must get out in the patio more often. I'll tell Ed I will water my plants this year. I'll make time for it, even if he offered to do it. I'll try to look as if my knees don't hurt.

I found things: new grasses sprouting. Daffodils coming up. Tiny green sprouts on the mock orange. A skinny tall tree that Mattie and Jack gave us was diverted from its skyward goal by the winds of winter. What could I do to help restore it to its former self? I like that tree with its branchless uprightness with a topknot of leaves: it could be a palm tree except that its leaves are nothing like palm fronds. I don't know what it is, but I've watched it grow in its own pot from a plant with its head below the garden lamp...a bit taller than I to a soaring statue with its crowning glory three times as high. I'll ask my neighbor Stewart next time he's raking the leaves what to do.

The dryer's gone off. I must have spent an hour in the blessed sunshine. I must stop my musing and get back to work.

The clouds let loose a shower of rain. But I've had an hour of thinking different thoughts, dreaming different dreams, an hour of honoring the coming of spring, an hour of soaking up the sunshine. I feel restored.

h

AN EMBARRASSING EVENT

Stomachs growl loudest in the sacred silence of a Quaker Meeting for Worship. I know that's true because mine was the growler that disturbed the meeting in Sebastopol last First Day.

Apple Seed Friends Monthly Meeting is the name of the local group of Quakers. Quakers are also known as The Religious Society of Friends, so Quakers equal Friends. Quaker members are called Friends, but attenders who are not members are just friends, with a small "f." That is an insignificant confusion, but consider that Monthly Meetings, such as Apple Seed, meet every week, and quarterly meetings (when numerous monthly meetings congregate) take place three times a year. Sunday is called First Day. Friends proceed as "way opens," that is "having waited for guidance from God, avoiding hasty judgment or action, and moving ahead as circumstances allow." Since the early 1650's, Quakers have often been considered "peculiar" for the simplicity of their life style and their unequivocal passion for peace.

Apple Seed Friends is an unprogrammed meeting. There are some Quaker churches with a pastor, and a Sunday service with hymns sung, scripture read, and sermons offered—all very much like a typical protestant service. But others, like Apple Seed, have chosen to be unprogrammed—essentially an hour of silence broken only by brief vocal ministry. The idea is to sit in silence together making oneself available to hear God's voice.

Local Quakers meet at the barn-red community building in Libby Park in Sebastopol. It's a small group and last First Day when I arrived, a portion of the dozen people who attended were already seated in pillow-padded, metal folding chairs placed in a small circle. As I eased myself into the squeaky chair I could hear my stomach roil. No one's bowed head rose, so I believed I was saved by the chair-squeak. Nothing stopped the incessant, increasingly noisy grumble...nothing, not holding my breath, not taking deep breaths, not arms folded over to muffle the sound. What happened to "way opens" when I needed it most?

All I could think of was that people had come to sit quietly listening for the voice of God. And what did they hear instead? Embarrassed, I sat with my head bowed and my eyes closed.

So I prayed. While God was considering an answer, Amy, sitting next to me, touched my arm with empathy. I rolled my eyes but I dared not look around the circle. With my rumbly stomach and squeaky chair, I dismissed the thought of leaving the room: that would cause further disturbance.

Finally, near the end of the hour, my stomach settled leaving me grateful for God's intervention, however long delayed. I could look up at my F/friends again.

♄

BETTER THAN A HALLMARK

Yesterday turned out to be even better than I expected. It was a busy day with Quaker Meeting for Worship, an after-meeting study group, a matinee at the Main Street Theatre in Sebastopol, and dinner at Ann Baumann's house in Santa Rosa. Ann, Louise Gross, and I have season tickets to the plays at Main Street Theatre and Ann had asked Louise and me to have dinner at her house following yesterday's performance.

When Louise brought me home, she pulled into the driveway. As I fumbled for my keys, I noticed the outside light was on. "That's funny. I remember that I didn't turn on that light. Look. The whole apartment is lighted up." Usually when I'm out, I leave one small lamp on low, but now the apartment was ablaze with light. Louise said, "I'll wait here until you find out what's going on."

I turned the key in the lock and motioned to Louise that all was okay. It was just my kids. Son John who lives in Healdsburg was there. Son Tom and his wife Robyn, who live in Rohnert Park, were there. Nice to see them, but unexpected. Did I have a good time at Ann's house? Yes. How was the play? Fine. Did I have my cell phone with me? Yes. Did I have it turned on? No.

I was flattered that they were worried about me. We are regularly in frequent communication so they usually know my whereabouts. Somehow I had failed to let them know my plans for this day. John called Tom. "Have you heard from Mom? She hasn't returned my call." Tom replied. "She hasn't returned mine either." Back and forth they called. They called my neighbor: she didn't know where I was. Separately, they decided to come check. A quick look at my wall calendar revealed all, so they waited, expecting me to return from Ann's house about when I did. A little visit, a little reprimand about keeping my cell phone turned on, and we said good night.

My Mother's Day came a week early. Better than any greeting card—even the very best, remembering those bright lights shining in my apartment will always be a symbol to me that my kids care.

♄

CHICKEN MARBELLA

OR THE TRIALS OF ENTERTAINING WHEN YOU'RE 82

To: lindal@aol.com 5/3/02,

Linda and Jack Lockett, circa 2002

When I mentioned to you when you called that I couldn't decide what to serve my five luncheon guests on Thursday, I didn't expect an e-mail from you with the solution to my problem. Thanks for the Chicken Marbella recipe! It was a godsend. It looked so easy and since you're such a wonderful cook I knew it would be great.

In your e-mail today you asked: How was the chicken? Answer: Short version: 1) Everybody said the chicken was delicious and they had a good time. 2) I served ample wine which they drank while I mucked around in the kitchen, so 1) above was not surprising.3) I will make the recipe again. Long version: Counting on leftovers, I used the full five pounds of chicken. The recipe said the flavor enhances as days pass.

The menu was, I thought, simple. Chicken Bordello—whoops, I mean Chicken Marbella—and rice, fresh asparagus, and John's green salad. For dessert, Pat's chocolate pudding pie—with pecans I brought back from Georgia in December—served with Dreyer's (same as your Amy's) vanilla bean ice cream. For appetizers, fresh pineapple chunks, herbed goat cheese with little crackers, and the aforementioned wine. I was happy with that and had all the tasks organized so I could be a calm, relaxed hostess. Yeah.

After I had the apartment looking pretty tidy, I decided on Wednesday to improve the appearance of my area of the patio. It was fun, I potted and repotted, swept and scrubbed, and by the time I called it quits to go to Fircrest to buy the food, my legs were shaky. I used the cane Tom brought over a few weeks ago. My strength forsook me. I struggled to get in and out of the car. By the time I had found the pitted green olives (I had to settle for Californian as Spanish were not available), the capers, and all the other items on my list, and had absorbed the shock of the soaring prices of wine—by that time, my legs were so weak and hurt so much I was almost in tears. I felt so old! It was an effort to get the groceries unloaded and put away, but I completed all the tasks I had scheduled to be done that night, and went to bed exhausted but confident that all was under control. How wrong I was!

Awake the next morning long before the time my alarm clock was set to go off, I realized I had a challenge ahead. My legs weren't working well at all. My pace was slow to slower. I knew trouble was ahead when I checked the oven to see if the dessert was done, only to find it had done nothing. I had set the oven temperature at 150 instead of 400 degrees.

The guests were to arrive at 12:30. About 12:20 the phone rang as I stepped out of the shower. First time guest Fred said, "Alice and I will be twelve minutes late." "Good," I said. A few minutes later, Alice called. "Did Fred call you? I had a little accident this morning and I'm leaving Kaiser right now. I'll be at your place in about twenty minutes." At 12:30, hair brush in hand, I greeted Sharon and Anna. Next came Drudy, then Fred.

They busied themselves helping while we waited for Alice. All scrunched into my tiny combination kitchen/dining room with barely room to move around the table stretched to seat six, Drudy arranged flowers, Anna put crackers around the goat cheese, Sharon set out the glasses, and Fred poured the wine. I, somewhat befuddled, had no idea what I should do. Meanwhile, the chicken (oh yes, the chicken) which had long ago baked its 50-60 minutes, was staying warm and drying out in the shut off oven. Alice came with her left wrist bandaged. She had hit it with a swing of her tennis racquet. While my guests learned the particulars, I noticed that the fool-proof automatic rice cooker was not cooking. The lid wasn't quite closed so it hadn't built up any steam. Another wait!

Finally, with everyone seated, I started serving the plates. I took the dry, blackened chicken from the oven, inwardly sighed, and bravely put the chicken, with a few crusted prunes, shriveled olives, and unidentifiable capers on each guest's plate. Fortunately there was plenty of the richly flavored marinade with which my guests flooded their servings of chicken.

The conversation was lively and interesting, and my wonderful guests generously praised the food. I can't say for sure as I had drunk no wine, but I think it was the cabernet blanc that salvaged what I considered a culinary disaster. Five pounds of overcooked chicken goes a long way. I put the leftovers in the freezer and will martyr my way through them.

Since I have partially full jars of pitted green olives and capers on hand, and a one-time experience with Chicken Marbella, I will—when my legs feel better—try it again. But next time with only two or three guests, a stripped down menu, and no gardening the day before. Now that I've told you the whole story, I bet you're sorry you asked . Say hi to Jack for me. Love you, Dodo

CHOCOLATES AND BIRDSEED

John and Patsy have no excuse to forget their wedding anniversary—ever. Valentine's Day. They were married on Tuesday, February 14, 2006, in Santa Rosa, California.

Sort of sweet, I think—choosing Valentine's Day—for a couple in their fifties who've been together for the past seven years or so. John called me a couple of weeks ago to say they had decided to marry. Everyone knows how fond I am of Patsy,

John and Patsy's wedding day, 2-14-06

happy to have her in my life in any way, and especially pleased for her to be my daughter-in-law. I glowed with the good news.

They planned to be married at the County Clerk's. My idea of getting married at the County Clerk's office was that they'd stand at the counter, have some flunky read legalese to them; they'd sign their names, and leave. It wasn't quite like that.

Valentine's Day afternoon was warm and sunny and Sonoma County fields blazed with yellow mustard blooming in profusion in the midst of pastures gloriously green from the recent rains. It was a perfect day to marry. When my son Tom and his wife Robyn and I arrived, the rest of the wedding party were there — on time for the scheduled 3:15 nuptials. Joel and Chris dressed casually but neatly for their Dad's wedding; Patsy's sister, Evie, married to Wayne a few weeks ago in the same place, busied herself pinning flowers on lapels; Johnny, Patsy's brother from Oakland, and his partner David, and David's interpreter for the afternoon, Sherry Jo, signed conversations that made them laugh; and Sally, Patsy's long time friend, completed the list of guests. John and Patsy were just a tad nervous. I thought they looked well pleased with their decision that brought about this happy occasion. Fine chocolates from La Dolce V in Sebastopol packed in individual boxes were given to each of us and were enjoyed as we waited patiently for the representative of the County Clerk to come.

But we were not at a counter inside the building. We were at an arbor in a pleasant grassy area outside the administration building. While we waited I admired Patsy's choice of her wedding attire. She loves clothes, has classy taste, stays slender, and looked absolutely great in a soft pink blouse made of lace with narrow same-color ribbons threaded through. Her skirt was silk crepe with a flowing pattern in springtime colors; rectangles of the silk were sewed together making a flared A-line with some corners of the rectangles forming a staggered hemline. A long sheer silk scarf worn loosely around her shoulders coordinated the colors and style. She carried a bouquet of spring flowers and was the very picture of a lovely bride.

While I scrutinized Patsy's pretty clothes, most everyone else was busy getting their cameras ready. Tom set up two video cameras to catch his brother's wedding scene from different angles, others had digital cameras flashing and clicking nonstop. Robyn brought a pint-size pink tin bucket, with pink ribbons fastened on, and found a place to put it until the right time to toss the birdseed it contained.

Barbara from the County Clerk's office read the marriage rites. A tall woman with a pleasant composure, she wore a bright red jacket, and her voice was strong and clear. The statement she read was without reference to religion or spirituality, yet was thoughtful and spoke to universal values. "It's not these vows that make a marriage," she said. "It's you." At my request, the County Clerk's office faxed me a copy of the marriage ceremony.

Patsy and John accepted rings from each other, kissed, and were pronounced husband and wife. They stood smiling and serene as we showered them with congratulations and birdseed.

John's ring is his Dad's gold wedding band. John told me he and Patsy left the inscription Bob and I had engraved inside it. Theirs is in addition to ours. As for Patsy's ring, oh, it was pretty. A gold band, delicate and fanciful, with golden filigree laced all around—a ring just right for Patsy.

Later, we celebrated with a delicious dinner at Lucy's restaurant in Sebastopol, and a luscious chocolate wedding cake. The time had come for goodnight hugs and heartfelt expressions of loving best wishes for the newlyweds.

A perfect day ended and a new journey began, for Patsy and John—a honeymoon in Hawaii and a lifetime adventure together.

♭

SEAT 21E

My son Paul made arrangements online for my flight to attend his daughter Clare's graduation from Boston University. When I downloaded my e-ticket I checked all the details: United flight 178, May 18, 2007, nonstop from San Francisco to Boston, leaving SFO at 1:00 PM, Seat 21E. Yikes! 21E! Row 21 is 'way back in the plane! It means I'll have a stimulating view of the dull, gray wing of the airplane for the 3000 miles across the country. That is, if my seatmate in Seat F at the window doesn't obliterate the view by pulling down the shade.

That E in 21E makes it worse. Seat E on a Boeing 757, which is what I'm flying, is a middle seat. The middle seat is designed by professionals to provide space for the seat itself: no designer, supervisor, or executive at Boeing ever contemplated that Seat E would hold an actual person. They did not have me in mind for Seat E. I am an 87-year-old with legs ten years my senior, somewhat overstuffed, diabetic, arthritic female. I flinched when I visualized fitting me, my bulging purse, carry-on, sun hat, and my collapsible cane into that tiny, awkward space. I did not look forward to the pain and embarrassment of trying to fit me into an E seat.

Clare's graduation from Boston U, 2007

I can't fault my son — he couldn't book the tickets until I made up my mind to take the trip. Although I wanted very much to attend my granddaughter's graduation, I worried. Will I get too tired? What if my legs cramp? What if I can't wait? What if I fall? What if...? I saw the doctor before making my decision. Perhaps I'm overanxious, I thought, when blood pressure, heart rate and other vital signs were near perfect. The last deterrent was my fear that my needs would draw attention from my granddaughter. It was her big day. Clare convinced me she wanted me there, and my son assured me he would push me in a wheelchair over Boston's bumpy, old brick sidewalks and the Astroturf at Nickerson athletic field where the ceremony would be held. By the time I gave my son the go-ahead, there wasn't much choice. I could blame only myself for Seat 21E.

On boarding the plane, my worries materialized. As I walked the long aisle back to Row 21, I noticed the distance between rows significantly diminish. I fumed. It should be illegal to have seats so crowded together! Do people sue the airline for the back problems they get? If not, they should. When I got to my row, I was glad to see that the passenger seated in F, the window seat, was already settled in...and that passenger D had not yet arrived. That gave me a little wiggle room to stow my things. I collapsed my cane and put it in a pocket of my carry-on. I took out The Sun magazine I had saved to read on this trip. I trusted my straw sun hat was crushable as I laid it on top of the carry-on under the seat ahead. As I turned to sit down, I looked at my neighbor, an attractive woman half my age with friendly eyes. I felt comfortable so I said, "I hope we get along. We have a long flight ahead." "As long as you don't smoke," she said. It was the right light touch as we both knew no smoking was permitted.

The passenger in seat D was a man who acknowledged my presence, then opened a thick book which I couldn't help observe was filled with graphs and tables ... a clear sign there would be no casual conversation with him. My window seat companion had already curled herself into the frame of the plane for a nap. As I predicted, she had lowered her shade obstructing my view of the wing of the plane.

I pulled down my tray to hold my magazine...and to cover my lap so my seatmates would not know that I frequently exercised my legs and feet. Tense. Relax. Tense. Relax. Every few minutes, I'd start with my toes and work my way up. It's a way I've found to allay cramps and swelling when sitting for so long in such a small space.

Hours later, with hardly a bump in our ride in the sky, the stewardess offered lunch. I chose the $5 chicken salad box: tender, roasted chicken breast rested atop a mass of iceberg lettuce. Two tiny cartons of salad dressing lay in one of the compartments of the box, and the third held chunks of refreshing fresh fruit. The challenge was to eat it. With my elbows pressed firmly into my ribs, my wrists made u-turns to carry the food to my mouth. My fingers that held my fork clamped into tight balls. I put my fork down and tried to massage the pain out of them only to have them spasm into witch's claws. I kept my eyes on my food and my fingers: I didn't want to see my neighbors' reaction to my uncontrollable convulsions.

When my neighbor D got up, I glanced at neighbor F. She and I silently agreed to leave our seats to avoid clambering over each other later. F watched out for me on the long walk to the rest room, but the flight was smooth and I managed without mishap.

When she and I returned to our seats, we began a casual conversation that soon had us laughing. I turned my body slightly so I could see her more clearly. A brunette, she had long, dark eyelashes that gave her eyes a warm depth. Her skin shone with a radiant luster. If she wore makeup, it was so skillfully applied it was not apparent. Her smile was genuine and her teeth were good. She was a beautiful woman...and, I quickly judged, not a vain one.

We fell into such easy conversation I think it surprised both of us. We talked for hours...unlimited subject matter and with appalling candor. With each new discovery, we laughed, we giggled, we sighed, we cried...all in the privacy of Seats 21E and 21F. We were awesome, we had to admit. People don't share their lives as we did unless they are dear, intimate friends. Or unless they know they will never meet again.

When we landed, I disentangled myself from my seat and stood in the crowded aisle. I turned to her and said, "Good-bye, my no-name friend." I held back the tears as I made my way down the aisle. A wheelchair waited for me. It faced into the airplane. When I sat down, I could see my friend, several passengers ahead of her, trying to get my attention. When our eyes connected, she called out, "I'm Julie," I smiled and gave her my name., "I'm Dorothy." I said, as the wheelchair attendant maneuvered me toward the exit.

How could I ever have known Seat 21E would be the best seat on the plane?

CHRISSY AND THE SAUERKRAUT SORORITY

Pre Co-op, Santa Rosa, CA 1964

About forty-five years ago, some members of the former Berkeley Co-op who lived in Santa Rosa and its environs decided to start a consumers cooperative food market in Sonoma County. We spent several invigorating years actively organizing. We wanted well-informed dedicated members that understood the democratic principles of co-ops and who would support the store with their patronage once it began operations.

We supported our organizing efforts with one-day-a-month Food Fairs. We purchased Co-op label staple food items from Associated Co-ops, a cooperative food wholesaler in Richmond, set them up in a rented space, and with all-volunteer help, we sold the merchandise to ourselves and to the public at normal retail prices. We named ourselves Pre Co-op so people would know this is not how a real co-op operates. The difference between the selling price at the Food Fair and the donation of our labor created a fund we used for a newsletter and other member-building organizing costs. In the course of building what we believed to be a firm base for a successful cooperative, we found ourselves developing nurturing friendships.

Six hundred members strong, we opened a handsome new food store at the corner of Marlow and Guerneville Road in Santa Rosa. In a few months, what could go wrong did. In less than a year, the market was closed and Cooperative Consumers of Sonoma County, Inc., was no more. Now, having demolished the co-op's building to build their big box, Safeway operates a busy enterprise, on that bittersweet corner.

But the friendships carried on. The Sauerkraut Sorority is a small but tangible legacy of those challenging years. Ann Baumann, Chris Gardner, Mimi Holbek, Anne Mudge, Janet Nolan, Mattie Rudinow, Iris Twigg, and I, each contributors to

Some of the members of the Sauerkraut Sorority. Back Row: Janet Nolan, Dorothy, Chris Gardner. Front row: Ann Mudge, Mimi Holbeck, Ann Bauman, circa 1995

the co-op effort, lovers of sauerkraut, keep the light burning in our long-lasting friendship in our unique sorority.

It all started when I complained to Ann Baumann that my husband, Bob, went out to the workshop or the garden or the library, anywhere to get out of the house whenever I opened a can of sauerkraut. It's not that I wanted sauerkraut every day, but sometimes I'd get a real hankering for it. Ann offered a solution for my problem: I could have sauerkraut at her house. She invited me for lunch, serving lunch where she served me simply superb sauerkraut, the recipe her father, Gustaf Baumann, brought from Germany. Mixed with pork and prunes and served with buttery mashed potatoes it was a meal to savor, to remember, and to share.

Other co-op friends were included, and over the years we've met together, usually in February and most often at Ann's house, the menu is always the same: sauerkraut and mashed potatoes. An eclectic group, we've weathered the years with appreciation for being who we are.

Chrissy's the one with the outrageous stories, the laugh that won't stop; the one quick with feisty responses whose generous nature can't be repressed.

A few years ago when Chrissy was hosting our annual event, Mimi, late as usual and dithery, came into the kitchen where Chrissy was mashing the potatoes. Panting, frustrated, she sighed, "Tell me, any one of you, just tell me one good thing about getting old!" No problem for Chrissy. She turned from the stove and brightly replied, "Well, you can't get pregnant."

Ann, Janet and Iris have died. Mimi has moved to another state. Ann, Chrissy, Mattie and I still get together. We've shared a lot of our lives: deaths, departures, disappointments, and joys and concerns for each other and the each-others in the world. But no pregnancies. So far.

♄

DEALING WITH FEAR

We live in a society fraught with fear. Political propaganda pressures us to be afraid...of Muslims, of black men, of terrorists, of neighbors who might be terrorists--especially if they look like Arabs. We're told to be afraid, and we are. I do not exclude myself: I've wasted many hours feeling insecure and frightened for no good reason.

As a child, I was afraid of the dark. As a young adult living alone in Oklahoma City, Washington, D.C., and in Detroit, I sometimes ran from the bus stop to my apartment, even though no one was ever following me. Once, when my sons were preschoolers, news on the radio was that a man had just murdered someone in nearby Petaluma and I locked the house, kept the kids inside, and peered out the window for hours. The murderer never showed up at our house. Unexpectedly, it's only been these past few years, as a widow, that I have, thankfully, overcome some of my scaredy-cat feelings. I still lock my car, keep alert to my surroundings, and check at night to see that my home is secure.

I wish I could be more like my friend Louise. Last year, she traveled alone to Italy then joined an REI hiking group in Italy where she had a wonderful two weeks. She goes camping into the woods alone. She never locks her car, goes wherever she wants, and has this free spirit I so admire.

Last night I had dinner at Louise's house. She drove me home, but left her front door open with apparently no thought of danger. A stranger wouldn't even have to break in to enter. When we arrived at my house, she thoughtfully waited in her car until she saw that I was safely in my apartment.

It had been an unusually busy weekend for me, and I was glad to be home. After checking the answering machine and e-mail, I turned on the tube and dozed. Awakened by a phone call, I realized it was time for me to admit exhaustion and prepare for bed. Just as I do each night, I checked to see that the two doors in my apartment—the patio door and the front door—were securely locked. Satisfied that all was in order, I slept peacefully through the night.

This morning as I stepped from the shower, I thought I heard a knock on my front door. There it was, another knock. I threw on a robe and hurried to the door. Jingling my key ring in her hand, my next door neighbor said, "Dorothy, I thought you might want to know. You left your keys in the front door lock last night."

$36.10 DOWN THE DRAIN

This time last week I was busy making cookies for my granddaughter Ann. Ann is a sophomore at the University of Washington in Seattle and I had promised her cookies to share with her roommates and, possibly, to take with her when she was on the crew of a sailing boat this weekend. I had my work cut out for me:

I needed to get the cookies to her before she left for sailing. Theoretically, I reserve Mondays for writing, and Tuesdays for writing class, but this called for a makeover of that schedule. The cookies must be mailed by Tuesday, Wednesday at the latest.

I started Monday by making the dough for four kinds of cookies. Orange Drop Cookies, Chocolate Crackles, old-fashioned Chocolate Chips (not the huge ones...they are reserved for birthdays), and Jubilee Jumbles. All of them are old favorites at our house and I made them with no nuts or raisins to suit Ann's twenty-year-old tastes. Tuesday, I figured, if I skipped class, I could mail them to arrive on time.

Early Tuesday morning (to me, anyway) I started rolling the Chocolate Crackles in balls, then in powdered sugar. They're so good, but I ate only one of the four dozen I baked. Then I covered a cookie sheet with butter and put a pan-full of Jubilee Jumbles on that, imaging how good they would taste with a burnt sugar frosting that was to cover them. I made only one cookie sheet-full as I was distracted, from the task at hand, but nine minutes later when the timer went off, I took from the oven the flattest, all-run-together, totally unattractive, probably inedible cookies that resulted from my adding too much baking powder to the recipe. Three kinds will do, I thought, as I got the Chocolate Chip dough out of the refrigerator. No Major Difficulties with them, if you don't count the variation in color. The Orange Drop cookies were a snap, coming out rounded and cute just waiting for the frosting on top.

By that time it was noon. I should have been able to cook them, enclose them in plastic bags, fill the box, and walked to the post office to mail them. I go a little more slowly these days, but I never seem to plan for it. By the time I got the box filled, the P.O. was closed. All I had left to do was put the address label on the package.

I could not get the computer to print the label. After wasting at least an hour Wednesday morning on that, I completed my handmade one which cautioned: THIS SIDE UP, FRAGILE, and PERISHABLE

I loaded it in my walker, and hurried downtown, and waited in line at the post office. When it was my turn, I told the clerk, "This needs to arrive in Seattle by Thursday afternoon." "That will be $36.10," she replied, but she gave me a moment to absorb the shock. "It's guaranteed to get there by noon tomorrow."

Waiting until Ann was home from work (She works at a hospital while

going to school.), I explained to her it would arrive but she didn't need to sign for it. She said it would go to an office with a staff person attending, so it would be safe. She was excited because she and some roommates were signing the lease for a house for the fall semester Thursday night. She'd call me to let me know (1) if they got there and (2) if they were any good.

True to her word, she called. It was Friday afternoon. With her boyfriend, Andrew, en route to Victoria to the sailing race. "Oh, Grandma," she said, "I'm so sorry. I forgot the cookies." It seems she got home too late after signing the lease, and the room was locked. She rushed to class Friday morning, then to meet Andrew and she forgot the cookies.

$36.10 for stale cookies!

♭

A FLOWER IN THE WRONG PLACE

Dull. Now, that's a harsh, judgmental word to use about a person, but it was my first impression of Anne. Shy and dull. And there. Always there. At every meeting. A dull, weedlike presence.

In the early 1960s Anne and I were members of a small volunteer group in Sonoma County. We shared tasks for an open house once a month. When it was Anne's turn to be hostess, she placed a straight-back chair facing the exact center of the entry door, six feet or so inside the room. She sat down, solidly set her feet side by side, straightened her skirt, laced her hands together on her lap, and stared straight ahead. I imagined her silent prayer. "Oh, God, please don't let anyone come while I'm here." A shell of silence was her protection from strangers. The task was torture for Anne, yet she sat there, tenaciously, until her replacement came.

My heart ached for her, but I was not drawn to her. A tiny person, her timidity shrank her into near nothingness. When Anne spoke it was with such a tremulous voice that she was either not heard or, if heard, ignored. She wore a lackluster brown wig. Except for a largish well-powdered nose, her facial features were unremarkable. Inconsistent with her otherwise bland persona, her clothes were lavishly colorful. Pink was her favorite, but red, orange, and yellow weren't far behind. Anne had no family. She lived alone in the country east of Santa Rosa.

A recent retiree with time to spare, Ann volunteered to work with me on a holiday cookbook for our members: I did the typing and she did the art work. I was not keen on the collaboration, but her lively, lighthearted drawings revealed an Anne I could not have envisioned. Simple stick figures came to life on the printed page. Impish little people sparkling with Christmas cheer were a clue to me that beneath Anne's dull exterior a spirited soul dwelled within.

Thus began a long friendship. Although petrified by shyness in most social settings, Anne relaxed with an eclectic group of supportive friends who shared her interests, valued her insights, and relished her sly humor. I was privileged to be among those friends. We worked on many projects together. Our family enjoyed potluck parties at her home. I remember lunches of Salade Niçoise which she served under the fig tree in her front yard: the persimmons she shared with us.

Anne created a Peaceable Kingdom on her acre. She loved cats and birds. By severely cutting back the vegetation from trees and bushes, the cats were always visible and the birds flew away at will. When a neighbor complained about Anne's unmanicured acre, Anne was not shy. "I like it natural. That's why I live in the country!" A linguist, photographer, nature lover, walker, reader, and an accomplished artist, Anne pursued many interests. She played the piano. A bit eccentric, she kept track of purchases to be made and chores to be done by placing messages to herself on the floor near the kitchen door where she couldn't miss them as she walked out to the garage. Throughout her long life—she died at ninety-three—Anne struggled with the curse of shyness. To those of us who knew her pain and loved her well, even her shyness was endearing.

Late in our friendship, when Anne was in her eighties, she told me of continuing, frightening nightmares about her mother. In the early 1900s, her sophisticated mother swirled in Sonoma Valley's high society where she was admired, adored perhaps, for her beauty and wit, her charm and social graces. Anne, her only child, did not meet her mother's expectations. Not acceptably "pretty" and painfully shy, Anne was a weed in her mother's perfect garden. Her mother often told Anne of her shortcomings and frequently sent her away to school or to travel where she would not be an embarrassment to her unloving mother.

What is a weed but a flower in the wrong place? Rest in peace, dear Anne.

♮

GRAY DAZE

There's an old-time expression I grew up with in Oklahoma that describes my plight exactly. I'm not sure that it's a uniquely Oklahoman saying or if my mother brought it with her from the smoky mountains of Tennessee, or my father from the rugged plains of Texas. It's part hillbilly and part Texas twang—but it's all truth to me on these gray wintry days here in northern California. "My git up and go has got up and went."

When my 1989 Nissan Maxima, worn down by its 220,000-mile history, decides not to start, I simply call AAA emergency and within the hour it's given a little help and is on the road again. I need something like that for my personal engine. I'd like a direct connection to the sun: a hole in the cloud cover to get me started for the day. I'm exhausted with doing nothing.

I know. I shouldn't complain. Most of the world has worse weather than ours most of the time. Especially now; with the tragedy of the giant tsunami, the eastern coast of the United States in blizzard conditions. My granddaughter's classes at the Boston University have been cancelled because of the massive snowfall there. And I have the arrogance to permit myself to suffer from gray sky inertia.

The fact is I am a sunshine person...not in the sense of being a bright little ray of sunshine bringing joy to all I meet, but rather as one who thrives in the bright light of a sunshiny day. When the morning skies are gray, it's hard for me to get started. If, perchance, the sun peeks through the clouds in late afternoon, it's too late to try. When the gray overcast hides the sun, I live in a stultifying daze of ennui.

One gray day last week, Dr. Morse gave me the advice I would want from a good doctor. He told me what I could do for myself to alleviate the symptoms of diabetes and arthritis; he urged me to do what I know I need to do to avoid further medication or surgery. Instead of being grateful, I came away from his office in tears, feeling inadequate to the task of accepting that responsibility.

I had to sit down and give myself a serious lecture. If the doctor's admonition had come on a bright, clear sunshiny day, my response would have been to pitch in with renewed energy to take charge of my health. How can I rid myself of the gray day daze that could lead to depression?

Within myself, I have the solution. I am a sunshine person, and I am also a person of faith. I know the sun is there. I will give myself a little easy space, relax in reverie on my unproductive days, and buzz like a bee when the sun comes out!

PAT AND THE PICKLES

Dear William,

Would you like to hear a funny little story about your great-grandmother and the pickles? I remembered it just this morning when my thoughts were flitting around trying to find a place to land. They buzzed about and plopped right on the pickles...and I thought to myself: oh dear, William will never know the story about Pat and the Pickles unless I tell him. (From now on in this letter, I am going to call your great-grandmother Pat, because she is my sister and it is a lot easier to type "P-a-t" than it is to type "g-r-e-a-t g-r-a-n-d m-o-t-h-e-r.")

When I was five, like you are now, Pat was in high school. When I was eight, she had moved to a different town to be a teacher. I liked having her for my sister. She laughed a lot, and she was very smart. People talked about how bright she was so, of course, I thought she knew everything.

One day when she came home for a visit, the family was sitting around just visiting and somehow we started talking about pickles. Which kinds we liked. Were Heinz pickles the best? And things like that. Then someone said, "You have to have a good cucumber to make a good pickle." Pat said, "Cucumber?"

"Yeah, cucumber. If you don't have a good cucumber you can't make a good pickle." "Oh," Pat spoke in a soft, timid voice. "I didn't know pickles came from cucumbers."

What did she think they came from? Did she think you could walk in a garden and pick pickles? Oh, this row, you see, is sour pickles. And that one is dill, and the next sweet. Ohhh, I don't think you can grow pickle relish.

Fortunately, Pat laughed a lot—even at herself. After the first embarrassment wore off, the whole family, including Pat, made light of it. Pat may not even remember it now. Next time you see her, ask her about it. She may tell you her memory of it, and it may be different from mine.

At least I learned that even very smart people don't know everything all the time.

♄

WHERE'S THE BEACH BALL?

Sonja and Paul, circa 1984

The Northern California setting was idyllic. A perfect Sunday in June, blue skies, moderate temperature, gentle breeze, California cuisine for lunch on a deck with a view of Sonoma Mountain and the hills east of Santa Rosa—it was a setting true to the concept of "The American Dream," and our family was living it up. On that day, Paul, our youngest son, and his wife, Sonja, had driven from Sacramento to spend the day with us at our home in Sebastopol.

On our return to Sonoma County in the early 1980s, we rented an upscale home, complete with swimming pool, on Fircrest Avenue in Sebastopol. It was there on the deck—between the sliding glass doors to the family room and the sparkling pool (pool maintenance was provided in the rental agreement)—that we lunched and luxuriated in the delights of family and the California life. Post-lunch inertia forced us to abandon the deck for less strenuous pursuits.

Patio and swimming pool at Fircrest house.

Sonja and I lazed about in the pool, on our backs with our elbows tucked into the gutter holding us to the side of the pool, our legs scissoring gently to keep us afloat and occasionally kicking at a big red and yellow beach ball as it came our way having been tossed along by the afternoon breeze and by the waves created by the varying intensity of our leg motions.

We talked a little—she told me about her studies toward a Masters in Public Health at Sacramento State University, and Paul's first job as a physical therapist at Kaiser Permanente Hospital in Sacramento, and I brought her up to date on Bob's and my activities at R&D Products. Mostly we just took it easy, the same as Paul napping on the floor in the family room and Bob snoring away on the living room sofa.

I interrupted the calm by calling out, "Where's the beach ball?" The next thing I knew, Sonja was peering through the shower curtain asking, "Dorothy, are you having a lovely shower?" "Well, yes, I am," were the words I spoke. But I was thinking, what in the world is going on? Why would she be sticking her head in while I'm taking a shower asking such a silly question? What happened between my question, "Where's the beach ball?" and Sonja's intrusion of my privacy in the bath goes like this:

Something in the tone of my voice alerted Paul from his nap. Instantaneously, he appeared at poolside to see what was going on. I swam over to the ladder where he stood and he offered me his hand to help me out of the pool. I walked to a table on the outer deck where I had left my scuffs, towel, and eyeglasses. I put on my glasses and scuffs, threw the towel around my shoulders, walked across the bridge at the lower end of the pool to the deck next to the house, and then walked through the family room, down the hall and into the master bath. I rinsed out my bathing suit and stepped in the shower. It was then that Sonja, concerned for my safety, checked to see that I was all right. She, Paul, and Bob had monitored my behavior. Their monitoring and my behavior were both unknown to me.

As for the beach ball, it was hidden in the shrubbery by the fence where either the wind or a strong kick had hurled it out of the pool into hiding. That was over. I was back in the real world. I felt fine. Paul thought I should see a doctor at Kaiser. I demurred saying I'd check it out on Monday. After all, Paul and Sonja had come over from Sacramento and it would take away too much of our day together to go to Marin County, the closest Kaiser at that time, and the rest of the family would be over later for dinner. But Paul insisted.

He drove me to the Kaiser clinic in Marin. We waited a long time for a young doctor in Emergency to see me. We waited an even longer time for the young doctor to diagnose what was wrong with me. The doctor left the examining room for such an extended period I suspected he was poring over books in the medical library. Whatever he did while we waited, he figured it out.

The doctor told me I had experienced an episode of Transient Global Amnesia (TGA), a temporary and isolated memory disorder. Most TGA patients are over fifty years old (I was 64) with an annual incidence of 23.5 per 100,000 in that age group. My episode was shorter than the mean of 4.2 hours. I was told, except for the absent memory, I was neurologically intact, and, like most, I did not lose semantic memory (memory of knowledge about the world, including the meaning of words and objects) or metamemory (awareness of what one should know). One of the precipitating factors includes swimming in cold water. Like other TGA patients, I was unable to recall the incident: I only know what Paul, Sonja, and Bob told me. I was heartened to learn I would probably never have another attack, although the incidence of a recurrence ranges from 1 month to nineteen years. That was twenty years ago, and the only aftereffect of that experience is whenever I can't find my car keys or forget to warm the rolls for dinner—or for any normal divergence from perfection—one of my sons is apt to say: "Mom, where's the beach ball?".

♮

THOMAS' ETAL

Thomas, age 3

Thomas speaking: "Well." With a long, drawn-out "w-e-l-l," three-year-old Thomas began his story. I could sense his imagination getting in gear as he took a deep breath and rolled his big brown eyes to the ceiling. "It was in E-gypt. A camel, a raccoon, and a pumpkin thought they would go to visit a friend. They walked along. They were hot. The camel, the raccoon, and the pumpkin got in some water. Then they got out and walked along. They met a goat. The goat was hungry. So the camel, the raccoon, the pumpkin, and the goat went to their friend's house. They loved being at their friend's house. The end."

Last week when I visited family in Richmond, Virginia, I took along little finger puppets (decorated for Halloween which was only a few days away) for my great-great nephews, William, who is six, and Thomas, three, just a few months away from four. As I didn't know which puppet would suit which child, I hid them behind my back. Thomas chose first: he got the raccoon and William got the goat.

The three of us sat close together on their grandparents' soft leather sofa and I told them a story my Daddy used to tell to me.

Daddy was a master at telling scary stories. At least they scared five-year-old me. This one was about his walking home on a dark, autumn night. (This was 1925 in Duncan, Oklahoma.) He carried a leather bag holding the day's cash receipts from the Sunshine Mercantile Company. Our house was only a few blocks away from his store, but the unpaved path was lined with elm trees making the dark night even darker. Daddy made a crunching sound as he walked on the dry fallen leaves. He thought he was being followed because he could hear that same crackly, crunchy sound behind him. He listened carefully. He was scared when that crunch crept closer. He held his money bag closer to his body, and his muscles tightened with fear. He quickened his steps: the crunching behind him kept pace. Bravely, he turned to face his tormentor only to discover it was a big old Billy goat just wanting to be friendly.

Now that I had told a story about a goat, William wandered away. But Thomas wanted one about a raccoon. I quickly manufactured a short one not worth retelling.

Then I asked if he would tell me a story.

That's when the big "well" came in. "Well." The prelude to his marvelous story. How could his three-year-old mind spontaneously place the raccoon and goat into a hot Egyptian setting with its natural inhabitant, the camel? It didn't bother Thomas that the legless pumpkin could swim and walk with his companions. Best of all was the ending: "They loved being at their friend's house." Here, I thought, is a child who is loved, who knows what's important.

So, I end my story with an admiring thank you to Gregg and Steve, topnotch parents, and to Thomas for telling me his enchanting tale of the camel, the raccoon, the pumpkin, and the goat.

♄

LETTERS

As told to me by Pat Markley, the Great-Grandmother, at 93.

Thomas and William, circa 2003

Great-Grandmother: "Do you have team sports in your kindergarten, William?"

William (5 going on 6): "What do you mean "team" sports?"

Grandmother (60ish): "Maybe it's called PE at your school. Do you have PE, William?"

Thomas, 3, interrupts: Thomas (proudly): "We have H and M at my preschool".

Grandfather (60ish): "Oh? What are H and M, Thomas?"

Thomas: "Well. We have lots of letters at our school!"

MY GUEST TOWEL DILEMMA

There's nothing I enjoy more than having friends in my home. I love them. I welcome them. But how come they don't use my guest towels?

I believe in the germ theory. How am I to know which towels to wash if there's no indication that they have been used? Not a towel out of place, not even a wrinkle as evidence of hands having been washed or dried.

Let's say I have a few friends over for lunch. During the course of the afternoon, one or more of them excuse themselves and go to the bathroom. Later, when my guests have left, I laze about in the afterglow of the pleasure of their company. Later, I wash the dishes and put the napkins and mats or tablecloth cloth in the laundry. Then on to the bathroom. Nine times out of ten that bathroom looks exactly as it did before my guests arrived, not a single thread on any guest towel molested.

It's a mystery to me. From the time I was a little kid I was taught to wash my hands after going to the bathroom. I assume that others have had the same hygiene instruction at home and at school. After all, this is the United States of America. What do they do if they don't use the guest towels? Wave their hands in the air? Wipe them on their petticoats? (Who wears petticoats these days?) Or use my personal towels I have already used?

It makes no difference whether I lay the neatly folded little terries on the counter top or nestle them in a basket, they don't attract users. Sometimes I've tried to overwhelm with quantity: guests towels on the counter, on the towel bar near the wash basin, on the one near the window, and with a basket of pretty little towelettes on the toilet tank top. Doesn't work. I have blatantly used towels with the word "Guest" carefully cross-stitched on them. I've hidden my own towels or taken them away completely. No luck: the guest towels still lie or hang unsullied.

Everything about my little apartment is California casual. There's no possibility a guest could imagine that leaving a used towel on the counter would offend me in any way. Yet there it is — my friends rarely use a guest towel.

When I asked my son Tom about this oddity, he quickly — and flamboyantly — demonstrated for me how he avoids showing that he's used a guest towel. By carefully slipping one wet hand underneath the fringe of the towel to the folds at the back, he gently wiggles his fingers to dry them on the back cloth, removes that hand, and repeats for the other one. No one, looking at the pristine front of the towel, will know that it's been corrupted. Before he finished his demonstration I knew he was just teasing me, but it did illustrate a possible reason for my guests' strange behavior. They simply don't want to cause me any work—like adding a little towel to the laundry? They should not worry about that. When I see no sign of guest towel use, I wash the whole bunch of them! No guest of mine will ever need fear that the towel offered is not a fresh, clean one.

I refuse to believe that my lovely guests do not wash their hands after going to the toilet. I will not put up a sign advising "Guests must wash their hands before returning to the dining table."

On those rare times when I can, I say a silent "thank you" to those few but thoughtful guests who leave a tousled towel in their wake.

♄

REMARKS FOR JACK RUDINOW'S MEMORIAL SERVICE

June 19, 2004

Mocha almond fudge was one of Jack's favorite ice creams. When I was shopping yesterday, that flavor dominated the space in the ice cream freezer, demanding that I buy a carton. I did, took it home, and treated myself to a delicious serving...in memory of Jack. Thank you, Jack, for happy memories.

Jack had a sweet tooth. It was my pleasure for forty plus years to have some baked goody—a spice bar, fudge drop or cookie—to serve when he and Mattie came by.

Many of our happiest family memories are the good times we've had with the Rudinows, and many of those memories had to do with food. We were often on the receiving end when they brought us some of their fresh garden produce...and it wasn't just zucchini either. They introduced us to guavas and Bob, especially, was more than willing to relieve them of the oversupply when their crop was good.

There was the time their freezer malfunctioned and Jack called to see if we could use some blueberries that would spoil if not used promptly. Of course we would help. Little did we know there would be a bushel of berries...at least it seemed like it. Bob and the boys rounded up neighbors and friends and I busied myself in the kitchen. It was a Sunday full of feasting on blueberry blintzes with sour cream and sausages, thanks to Jack and Mattie.

Mattie and Jack Rudinow, circa 1998

We had the good fortune to meet Jack and Mattie during the first year we were in Sonoma County. They were among the twenty-eight Berkeley Co-op members living in this area who decided, in early 1960, to develop a successful cooperative food store here. For six years we functioned as PreCo-op, educating and organizing toward that goal. When we opened the store as Cooperative Consumers of Sonoma County, Inc., there were 600 members. When the store closed less than a year later there remained bittersweet memories and long-lasting friendships. Keeping the books, dealing with incorporation, putting cans on the shelves at the monthly Food Fairs, Jack worked on that project with the same diligence and competence he demonstrated in any task he undertook. We all counted on him; his good nature was a bulwark in times of stress.

His good nature and gentle spirit showed itself in many ways. When Joel and Ann and Dita were young, he called them in from the farm to supper, or for whatever reason, not with a holler or a clang, but with a musical three-note whistle. That whistle was and is to me a symbol of the right way to raise kids.

One of Jack's attributes was the quality of his listening. He followed Bob's invention, patenting and production of the Call Back Message holder with sustained interest. As the time neared to market Bob's initial idea-to-market invention, Jack said he wanted to buy the first one. "No way," Bob told him. "I'll give you one or as many as you can use. You can't buy one from me." Jack insisted. He wanted to be our first customer. Bob quickly estimated the total cost of development of the product, and offered it to Jack at the ridiculous price of thousands of dollars to cover those costs. Jack didn't go for that, and he paid us the retail price of $1.98 plus tax to buy the first creation of R&D Products.

Jack's facility with figures is well known. He was treasurer or kept books or financial records, to my knowledge, for the co-op, sometimes for R&D Products, for our son John's brief JambTite endeavor, and for HealthWatch, the group that tried to monitor Sutter's compliance with its hospital contract with the county.

In his work with the Sonoma County Water Agency, Jack was knowledgeable about laws and practices relating to real property. All of you know that Jack Rudinow was a serious person given to rational, practical behavior. I have in my hand a copy of a legal document that belies that knowledge. It is a Quit Claim Deed "in consideration...of love and affection... zero dollars," in which he assigns to his heirs "all of land situated on the moon and overlooking the County of Sonoma, bounded and described as follows, to wit: Beginning on the moon at the intersection of latitude 54 North with longitude 12 West..." and on for five more lines of land description, ending with: "Containing 128 square kilometers of land, more or less, and containing all of Crater Plato." Signed and witnessed July 19, 1983.

Jack was a good person who worked hard to make life better for everyone. I never knew how serious he was about it, but when the politics of our American-style capitalistic society wore him down, he talked about moving. To Canada? Norway? Nope. Too cold. Wherever Jack chose to go, I hope there's a socialistic/cooperative economic system: I think that would suit him just fine.

I'm not too much into heaven and hell, but everywhere, with my eyes and in my soul, I see evidence of the continuum of life. Wherever there's an act of kindness, Jack's legacy is there.

JACKSON

Dorothy and Jackson, circa 2001

On unusually cold nights in Sebastopol, Jackson, the cat given to me and Bob by Tom and Robyn as a kitten, was allowed to stay in. Last night, however, it wasn't quite so cold when I told him time to go out. He prolonged the ritual, as he rearranged himself on the plaid blanket in front of the wall heater. When he finally made up his mind, he walked toward the front door, then stopped halfway through to think about it some more. Then he proceeded to the door to be let out. It was colder than I thought.

Tonight, after getting his nightly back rub and sitting on my lap for a spell after I'd had my supper watching TV, I noticed Jackson wandered around the room. He curled up on the plaid blanket as usual, but went to a dark corner under the rocking chair as if he were hiding. Not a sound from him while I watched News Hour and checked out the Charlie Rose program to see who was being interviewed. As I turned off the television and the lights, I said, "Jackson, OK, time to go out."

Total quiet.

I opened the door: the air felt like Oklahoma or Pennsylvania or other really cold places where I've lived. Jackson was hiding, didn't want to be noticed. Maybe I'd think I let him out earlier!

Now I'm ready for bed, satisfied to be a part of Jackson's scheme. I'll gladly get up when he scratches gently on the chair by my bed about five tomorrow morning.

♄

LOVE, SWEET LOVE

According to the doctors, my brother Dub should be dead by now. Last year, in September 2003, he was diagnosed with stomach cancer with the prospect of living for perhaps six to eight months.

A few months before, in April 2003, Dub drove from Roanoke—where he lives at the Methodist Retirement Home—to Richmond, Virginia, to see our sister Pat. I was there at the time having come from California for the same purpose. Pat, at 93, was frail and with constant arthritic pain, but she was feisty and good company. Even so, each visit was always with the apprehension it could be our last.

Walter Lockett, Green Church, Roanoak, VA., 2003

Dub seemed in good shape then—especially for a 94-year-old. We stayed with Pat's daughter and her husband in their fancy, high-ceilinged home with its long, wide staircase to the second floor. When I returned to California, I told my family how Dub showed off—bounding down the stairs like a teenager. He thrived on ritual, as a Methodist minister and in his personal life, exercising vigorously and faithfully with daily gym work and walking. It paid off as his physical and mental abilities were those of a much younger person. He did confess to having some little health problem, but was so vague about it I assumed it was a temporary traveler's complaint, diarrhea or constipation, and nothing was made of it. It didn't hamper his affability as he fully engaged in conversation and activities, but he excused himself frequently...sometimes to make phone calls.

After each phone call, on returning to the family group, Dub wore a sly smile. Uh oh, we thought, he's at it again. We soon learned his calls were to Charlotte Meyers, a long-time friend and widow of a fellow Methodist minister. She lives at the retirement home where Dub lives. They were arranging dates to see a play in Roanoke and to make a trip to a Methodist conference later in the spring, taking a stopover at our brother Jack's home in North Carolina. The frequency of the calls convinced Pat and me that Dub was courting Charlotte.

Helen, Caroline, Gaylord and Walter

Dub has a penchant for romance. He was married to Helen, his college sweetheart and a woman whose looks and elegant good taste reminded me of Wally Simpson. Dub was no Duke of Windsor but he and Helen seemed happy in their marriage and as parents of two fine children, Caroline and Gaylord. When Helen's poor health required several years of intensive care giving, Dub gave it with devotion. Helen died when she was sixty.

Within weeks of her death, Dub was surveying the scene for a new wife. The view from the pulpit was rich with opportunity: a mass of eligible widows and unmarried women filled the pews. Letters from Dub told of the virtues and perceived imperfections of women he took to lectures and concerts and to the theatre. When a church-related conference took him to New York, he asked Virginia, a sixty-year-old unmarried woman who was an administrator at the Methodist headquarters there, to attend a play with him. They exchanged visits over the next few months.

Virgina and Dub

On returning from New York one night, he wrote her a letter. "Dear Virginia," he said, "I am looking for a wife." He went on at length about the attributes he desired in the woman he'd choose to be his life-partner. When Virginia received it, she immediately sent him a telegram. "STOP LOOKING." They were soon married. Virginia was a robust woman—talkative, full of laughter and common sense. A dozen or so years later, when my husband and I were visiting them in Roanoke, our conversation led to a discussion of death and dying. Virginia commented, "I know exactly what Dub will do if I die first. He'll waste no time looking for another wife!" Dub devoted his life to caring for her during her last years as she lay bedridden and befuddled with dementia. Virginia died in October, 2002. She was 93.

It was no surprise that Dub started looking again, but his search was unexpectedly delayed. Not long after our April visit last year, Dub's traveler's complaint turned out to be bleeding ulcers.

"You nearly bled to death," the doctor told him. Concurrently, he suffered excruciating back pain, and while doing tests for that, it was discovered he had advanced stomach cancer. That's when the doctor told him he had six to eight months to live.

By this time, Dub had celebrated his 95th birthday. He was not a suitable candidate for back surgery and, at his age, he chose not to have chemo or radiation treatments for the cancer. An injection of a liquid cement around his spine stabilized the area, relieving the pain-causing intervertebral disk compression. He moved from his studio apartment to the skilled nursing facility at the Methodist home, signed up for hospice care, and savored each new day of a professionally predicted shortened life. In early October, my brother Jack and his wife Linda drove from their home in North Carolina to see Dub. On October 11th, 2003, they e-mailed the family, "Dub is stoic and strong and still tries to do as much as he can for himself and remain upbeat. We do not know if we will see Dub again. If any of you plan to visit him, we suggest that you do it sooner rather than later."

Charlotte and Dub, 4-16-04

With that advice, son Tom and I coordinated with my youngest brother Hoyl in Kansas City and flew to Richmond. There we borrowed my niece's van; put in Pat, her wheelchair, walker and portable toilet riser; and headed south to Roanoke. There we found Dub gaunt (he had lost 38 pounds), tired, and in love. We met Charlotte and all agreed she's lovable. Only 89, she's attractive, articulate, agile and nurturing. Her attention to Dub's needs, and her obvious fondness for him warmed our hearts. Pat, without subtlety, asked Dub "How would you describe your relationship with Charlotte? Platonic?" "No," he answered. "Affectionate."

That trip was the last time we saw Pat. She died in January this year. In planning a family memorial service for her mother, Pat's daughter Susan knew that Dub could not safely travel to Richmond, so she arranged with him to have the ceremony in Roanoke. Friday, April 16, 2004, sixty Lockett family members and Charlotte Meyers, were guests of Dub at the Roanoke Methodist home where Dub, sharply dressed in his crisp white shirt, proper tie and light blue jacket, greeted each of us by name and with gusto. Charlotte said he was invigorated by our presence.

We had dinner there that night and lunch on Saturday. After lunch, we celebrated Pat's rich life in an untraditional, often lively memorial service, and spent the rest of the afternoon in conversation clusters or, age and energy willing, playing Frisbee . I sat next to Dub at our special dinner that night at the old Roanoke Hotel. Charlotte was nearby: he wanted her to switch seats to be next to him. While I feasted on the hotel's gourmet food, Dub opened his brown paper bag and ate soda crackers and a banana. He told me he had a doctor's appointment in a couple of weeks to check the progress of the cancer.

When I called to see how the tests turned out, he crowed, "I don't have any cancer. They could find no tumor. I've gained back 24 of the 38 pounds I lost. I'm walking over a quarter of a mile a day and adding a little every day. They took back the walker. I've released hospice. I want to live. I want to be with Charlotte."

The family calls it "Charlotte's Miracle."

LATER: Biopsies show cancer still lingers in the lining of Dub's stomach. His daily walk is now up to a mile, his appetite is good; he's kept on the weight. Dub will be 96 on August 19th.

♄

STAYING FOCUSED

Today is Monday, December 8, 2003. My writing class meets this afternoon at 2:00 at the Sebastopol Area Senior Center. The SASC newsletter calendar for December notes that the class will be on Tuesday, but I know that is misinformation as our teacher, Suzanne Sherman, told us the class would meet on Tuesdays beginning in January next year.

I'm telling you all of this because when I awakened this morning I asked myself are you going to write about William being an "R" at the PTA meeting? Or, are you going to write about Dub's falling in love—at 95? Thinking about both stories at once made it difficult to decide, so I thought about something else. Shall I take a shower now, or after I write the story?

It takes me a long time to shower. I have a few things to think about before I get wet. One thought is am I too hungry to shower before breakfast? Will my blood sugar be low if I don't eat something now? It never has been too low, but I suppose it could be since I am diabetic. I took my blood glucose count, which requires exactly 45 seconds. That's my scheduled time for my daily exercises. I can't understand why my count is higher than usual this morning, but I note it on my BGC record card and put a big question mark by the number. I take off my pajamas and think I really should mend those little holes on the leg of my pajama pants where Jackson's cat claws landed when he leapt to my lap the other evening. If I don't mend them now they'll get bigger and big—no. No I won't. I'm cold. As long as I'm naked, I might as well weigh myself. I really like the new digital scales Tom and Robyn gave me. They're not exactly new. They're an extra T&R had. Why would they have an extra? I don't know. I didn't ask. When my old scale went kaput, they gave this one to me, and it tells me to the tenth of a pound what I weigh. That's not something I actually need to know, but I can be encouraged by a .2 pound weight loss. It takes very little to make me happy.

I love a hot shower. It might take less time to shower if I didn't enjoy it so much, and if I didn't forget which part I've already washed. You see, I have a system about scrubbing myself, and it works very well except sometimes I think about things like whether to write a story about William being an "R" or about the look in his eyes when Dub talks about Charlotte who is only 88. But I always go back. If I think I might have missed an elbow or a knee, I'll scrub it even if it's the second time around. I come out of a shower clean and hungry.

First, I thought, I'll have my breakfast and clean up the pans I'd used baking the pirajs for the potluck last night, then I'll write my story. I'm watching every digit on the new scales. I am on a new-to-me 40-30-30 weight loss program so I sliced an apple in thin strips, measured out 1½ tablespoons pure crunchy style peanut butter to dip them in, made a cup of hot Inka, and sat down to eat at the table in my cozy little kitchen. This is usually a time that brings me great pleasure. Each moment (as classmate Ron has helped me learn) is precious: the winter sun warms and nurtures me, the neighbor's voices are gentle, and Jackson's silent pleadings to please let me in make me feel needed.

But not this morning. The pans cluttered the counter space. Every speck of dust, every fingerprint on cupboards, every liver spot and freckle on my hands and arms was magnified, intensified by the blaze of sunshine that bore itself through the dirtiest sliding glass doors my neighbors have ever seen. And then I remembered: I can't a write story today. My printer is jammed.

When you consider that I am a handicapped person having been bribed by my grandmother to write with my right hand when I am naturally left-handed, you can understand my plight. It's been a burden all my life, trying to behave like a right-handed person. In business classes in high school, I learned to be a fast typist but I could barely decipher my awkwardly written shorthand notes. I could fake it with a good memory. I hated to write longhand so badly, I married because my love brought his old Royal manual typewriter to the marriage. Creativity blossomed for me with the advent of electric typewriters: the IBM Selectrics were like best, best friends. Now here I am this morning, totally adrift because I can't write a story on a piece of paper using a pen or pencil. I can put it on my computer, but I can't get it out.

I know exactly the size and shape of the bit of paper stuck in my printer as I have tried several times to remove it. John offered to help me and advised me not to move or lift my Hewlett-Packard combo fax-scanner-copier-printer. My sons keep telling me what not to do: it's often easier on them than if I try and don't succeed. But I decide to give it one more try. Simple. All I did was pull the H-P out from the wall, open a door, and there the jagged paper scrap was waiting for me. Simple, except that I pulled out too many plugs from the surge suppressor strip and then I could not sort out all the wires and plugs to put them together again. That obviously needed attention.

If you could see my desk right now, each and every plug is labeled correctly. No matter how many electrical cords are unplugged I can show you exactly to which device they belong.

But don't come see it today, as all the stuff I took off my desk is on my bed.

Having class on Tuesdays, I think, is going to work out fine for me. I can write my story on Monday (as usual), and then proofread it Tuesday morning. Maybe I can write about Dub and William all on the same day. What a great idea.

♮

TEACHING VALUES

Today I found the source of one of my mother's favorite expressions. Often, over the years, I have remembered the caution of her stilted words: "Comparisons are odious." Only this morning did it occur to me to that it might have come from something she memorized when she attended a female seminary in Tennessee in the early 1900s. There on page 83b of Bartlett's Familiar Quotations, 1955 edition, are the exact words written by John Fortescue in De Laudibus Legum Angliae in 1471.

Susan Alberta Ivins Patty Lockett

The word "odious" sounds like its meaning, hateful; it's a vivid word, one that's not easy to forget. She wanted us to accept our siblings, our relatives, our neighbors and friends, and the hoboes that knocked on our back door asking for food, as individuals, not to be rated in comparison to others. She taught us to be kind, not only with a powerful tool of language, but by example. Mother didn't gossip with her neighbors or her sisters, however ample the opportunity.

♄

CONNECTIONS

No more Wednesday night calls, Pat, not by telephone anyway. You died yesterday. It was on Sunday, a little before one o'clock in the afternoon, the 11th of January, 2004, at Henrico County Doctors' Hospital in Richmond, Virginia, several hours after you had another stroke. Susan and Bert, Gregg and Steve, and Laura (Parsons) were with you, surrounding you with their love, grief, and a flood of Lockett family tears.

Susan Patty Lockett Markley, circa 1930

I wonder how it is for you now, Pat. When you die, do you know it? You were so down-to-earth about death—so sure there was nothing after death. When you die you die you said. That's it. For all your years of teaching Sunday School classes, you chose your own creed. You spent more time caring for others than you did conjuring visions of life after death.

It would please you to know not a single person—so far, at least—has told me you passed, passed on, or passed away. No one has said Pat made her transition. Each person has been straightforward just as you'd like. They say to me, "I'm so sorry your sister died." One person did say, "I'm sorry for the loss of your sister." (And I thought, if you're lost can I find you?) All in all, you'd be happy with the way family and friends have been plainspoken about your dying. "Pat died." they say, "and oh, how we will miss her." I already miss you, the best big sister ever. Even so, I think you died at the right time.

My neighbor, the one who lives in the pink Victorian whose mother died last year, told me this story today. Her mother was 99 years old when she died. When she was 95, a friend asked her, "How is it being 95?" Her mother's reply was a terse, "I wouldn't recommend it." See how wise you were to die at 94!

Bert e-mailed the family to say you died of a hemorrhagic stroke. That was the fatal blow. Two weeks of unbearable arthritic pain, then the pneumonia, the inability to swallow, the edema. It was just too much, Pat. Your body wore out, but rest assured your mind kept going to the end. It did show signs of faltering a day or so before your death when Laura (your granddaughter) beat you at Scrabble, but you were quick at repartee when Laura (your niece) and Richard came to see you later.

One night when I called the hospital, Susan answered the phone. She wasn't having much success feeding you. She told me you had a rough day and might not feel up to talking with me. "Mother, it's Dodo on the phone. Do you want to talk with her?" You did, but your voice was so strained, so weak, I could hardly hear you. Tears welled in my eyes and I choked, "What can I do, Pat, what can I do to help you?" You whispered faintly, slowly, "Love me." Regaining my composure, I faked a light-hearted "Well, I'll try." You came back, barely audible but feisty. "Put a little effort into it."

Pat and Dorothy, Richmond, VA., circa 2003

It wasn't hard to love you. Howard married you, he said, for your gaiety and laughter. Your kids and their kids and their kids all loved you and showed it. You, more than anyone else in the family, nurtured and received affection and love from all our one hundred Lockett family members. Your enviable collection of antique celery vases paled compared with your abundance of friends. You reached out to people and reaped the reward of their love. Love you? How could I not love you when you were so important in my life? From giggles to tears, we shared our feelings...and politics, too!

Lucky, much-loved sister, now you are dead. I'll grieve for you, the tears will flow, my heart will ache, but unlike you, I am not so adamant about a nothing after death. I'm open to the possibility of continuing connections. Don't be surprised if you hear from me again.

♄

A PERFECT DAY

Have you ever wanted to write something but couldn't come up with a reasonable format for it? I have just such a story in mind, but it doesn't have a beginning, a middle and an end. It doesn't have a climax. Nothing happens really. And it was almost the most perfect day of my life.

My granddaughters, Clare and Ann, came to see me a couple of weekends ago. It was the last chance they had before school starts for Ann and before Clare goes back to her job in Alaska. Their home base is Gig Harbor, Washington. Ann's highlight of the summer was a sailboat race from Vancouver, B.C., to Maui, Hawaii, with scary high waves and a calm-at-sea making it a never-to-be-repeated experience. Clare set out on a summer journey with Diana, a roommate from college, that covered Athens, Rome, Paris, and Madrid. On the first day, Clare was mugged.

I love having them stay with me. My apartment is so tiny—at least it seems so when the living room floor is covered with their duffel bags and the bathroom counter seems to stretch to accommodate their cosmetic items. When we transform the sofa into a bed, we hopscotch over pushed-back furniture and pushed-around miscellany with high caution.

And so it was. The grandmother love was just as strong as when Clare was a toddler. As I put her down for her nap, I whispered ever so softly. "You're so pretty," In a sleepy voice, she answered, "I know." Now she's twenty-three, and I still get goose-bumps when I think of her fearlessness, her independence, her prettiness.

And Ann, with her Daffodil Princess smile, telling us one of her YWCA youngsters this summer guessed her age at forty. Ann will be twenty-one a week from now. I remember when she was three and she quit kneading her mother's elbow long enough to defend, successfully, the two handbags which were given her at Easter and shamefully coveted by Clare. My heart was with her then and I feel the same now admiring her fearlessness, her independence, and her prettiness.

One reason I believed I couldn't write about this perfect day is that I felt I didn't have the skills to describe the kind of day it was. I wanted to convey the way the ocean makes you feel powerful, very much in charge. Then you let go, your body and mind relaxed; you succumb to the sweet-ness of irrelevance. The TV show Laugh-In used to have a character, an adult who rode a child-sized tricycle on the beach and appeared on many of the shows. Each time he was on he would come high-tailing it down the beach, then suddenly plop over and be sound asleep in the soft sand: I could have been that trike rider.

The sun never quite shone through. Above the mistiness, it was always there, making you think it was going to come out...but not so you really thought it would. It was still a gray day...with the kind of coastal fog that makes an Oklahoman like me feel an unnatural comfort with it, that makes me want to run the long expanse of seashore all the while wishing just as much that I could lie down in the sand and take a nap.

Ann, Dorothy and Clare, Wright Beach, CA, circa 2008

That's how it was on Sunday afternoon when Clare, Ann, Tom, Robyn, and Chooey (their very large dog) and I went to the Sonoma coast. Chooey knows what to do at the coast. He goes crazy. Too much sand to dig, too much ocean to ponder, too much room to run. Clare and Ann go off with Chooey.

Robyn helps me plod through the sand to a place to have lunch. Tom carries in our picnic food and a chair for me. There's a cup-holder on the arm of the chair. I have my diet Pepsi while Robyn puts out our lunch of avocado and Havarti cheese sandwiches on the biggest, brightest beach towel ever.

We ate; we talked. Tom used Chooey as a pillow. We laughed. We hung out. That's about all we did. Nobody made any particularly bright remarks, no mishaps..

We went from there to John and Patsy's house where we ate grilled eggplant and zucchini because Clare and Ann are vegetarians. We played a new game called Apples to Apples which was fun even though I lost.

Chooey and Tom

Sounds of Clare on her cell phone and of Ann listening to late night TV seeped through the walls as I went to sleep thinking what a nice day we'd had: it ranked right up there as one of the very best. With the perspective of the 32,386 days I've lived, I'd call it a perfect day.

A QUIET PLACE

There are six apartments at The Wilton where I have lived for the past five years. Four apartments are in a two-story building with a small green space between the building and the sidewalk; the other two apartments are in the back above the carport. The Wilton is only two blocks from Main Street in Sebastopol. It's an easy walk downtown, but coming home requires climbing a fairly steep hill. It's a modest, pleasant place to live.

It's pleasant because the rents are moderate by Sebastopol standards, the landlord is unintrusive, and the tenants are friendly but respect each other's privacy. The sliding glass door in my kitchen gives me a close-up view of the comings and goings of my neighbors as they pass through our common patio to the carport. I adjust the vertical blinds to regulate the sun shining through or the privacy I seek. I like the sunshine and my neighbors so my blinds are most often open.

Tenants here have a tendency to stay. In the five years I've been here, there has been very little turnover. There have been the most changes in the apartment directly above me: Mary, a business consultant who worked from her apartment, bought a condo in Santa Rosa two years ago; then Vivian, whose politics matched mine, moved to the country when she retired; a restless young couple lived there a couple of months this summer, moved on without a word; and now, Ben and Evie, a young engineer and his wife, working on her master's degree at Sonoma State University, are a delightful addition to our mix. In the other apartments, there have been fewer changes. My greatest regrets for myself and happiness for them were when the two families with children moved to houses with yards. I wasn't too sad when the neighbor with the three neurotic cats left: my Jackson was a happier feline after a day or two of snooping around to make sure they were gone. One apartment had no turnover at all: Millie had lived here for thirty years. She died about three weeks ago. Millie's death saddens me; we had become good friends. I am now the tenant with the most seniority here, both in age and occupancy. I like living around people younger: the ages here are in the twenties, thirties, forties, fifties...and the eighties.

For the first time, I was the only tenant on the premises this past weekend. It was strangely quiet. My next door neighbor, Melissa, was back east attending a Buddhist gathering. Curtis was off to Canada to be on a TV game show, a show with two teams of writers challenged to write stories on a specific narrow theme selected by the audience. The stories were viewed on a big screen as the writers wrote them. Curtis was invited on the recommendation of the publishers of his first book due in bookstores in March. Gwen, who lives above Melissa, left Thursday for a job interview in Oregon. Having completed her master's in library science, the perfect job for her awaits in a high school library. She is passionate about encouraging teenagers to read and I'm holding good thoughts that she will be chosen...if it's what she wants. It's taken courage for her to apply as a job in Oregon means a significant change in the comfort level of living near her family. Ben and Evie were off to southern California for Evie's sister's wedding. Sounds from the apartment above startled me until I remembered Ben hired the ten-year-old girl across the street to care for their cats while they were away.

It surprised me to find myself lonesome for my neighbors. This weekend without them makes me appreciate them all the more. They'll get a fond welcome and an eager listener as they tell tales of their adventures.

♄

A VERSION OF THROWING OUT THE BABY WITH THE BATH WATER

The details were sketchy. Alicia left her apartment for class at Cal Poly last Thursday. In making a left turn onto a busy thoroughfare, a big SUV struck the passenger side of her sedan. An ambulance took Alicia to the emergency room at a hospital in San Luis Obispo. When Alicia's roommate called Karen, Alicia's mother, there wasn't anything more to say.

Anxious about Alicia's injuries, Karen found someone to take over her class . She called her sons and her father to tell them what she knew of Alicia's accident and to say she was leaving for San Luis Obispo. Her father, Ken, wanted to go with her to be with his granddaughter. In the late afternoon they headed south.

After an hour or so, they made a gas stop. While Karen tended to the gas, Ken purchased snacks and beverages from the mini-mart dispensers. He chose a large Dr. Pepper for Karen and placed it in the holder between the seats. On the road again, Karen, whose soft drink of choice is Pepsi, complained, "Daaad, you know I don't like Dr. Pepper." Karen cautioned herself to calm down as they had several more hours to drive...in heavy commuter traffic...in the dark...on roads only minimally familiar to them. With the hectic driving tension, combined with her concern for Alicia, Karen's stress level rose. They took a wrong turn, found themselves on an even busier freeway. With traffic more dense, the dark darker, and with no familiarity with their surroundings, Karen reached for relief...the cup full of soda in the console beside her. She grimaced when the first taste of Dr. Pepper touched her tongue. She rolled down her window, tossed out the soda, and put the empty paper cup back in its holder. That was the moment of the big uh-oh. She had tossed out her mandibular full denture with the Dr. Pepper!

Karen has worn full dentures for several years. Lately, the lower plate has not fit well. It hurts her gums so much she often, when alone, takes it out. Karen is a music and movement educator for preschoolers and drives a lot on her job. She developed the habit of putting her aggravating lower denture in a paper cup set in the beverage holder in her car. You know the rest: she had without thought—as is consistent with a habit—dropped her lower denture into the cup at her side. This time the cup also held Dr. Pepper.

Thoughts of making an attempt to retrieve the denture from the freeway would be the thoughts of a crazed, suicidal idiot. Although Karen dreads gumming her way through life for the six to eight weeks it takes to get a new mandibular full denture, she's able to take her loss in stride. She needed a new one anyway. As for

Alicia, the cuts on her pretty face required fifty or more stitches, but she, like her mother, is a trooper. She attended her chemistry lab the next day. The doctor on duty at the ER was a plastic surgeon: I'm told her stitches are beautifully done.

♮

MY POST OFFICE ADMIRER

A man I had never seen before looked right at me and said, "My, your hair is beautiful." I muttered a weak thank you and walked toward the line waiting for service at the Sebastopol post office.

My hair did look nice. I had just come from Carol Nelson's Main Street Hair Co. up the block—there is a gas station and La Taqueria, set back from the street, in between—and the salutary effect of the good haircut she gave me had not worn off. But why would a casual compliment from someone I didn't even know give me a warm feeling? Was I so in need of attention that I was touched by an idle remark from a transient (and he may well have been one...although he had short hair and no scruffy beard). Wasn't this the kind of thing that should set off an internal alarm? What was he up to? He looked about sixty, clean enough, dressed in blue jeans and a long-sleeved shirt with an open collar. He didn't look evil...but, still, these days...

After I had been waited on and as I turned to leave the building I saw my hair-admirer standing by the door. He opened it for me; I nodded my thanks. I walked down the steps on one side of the handrail, he on the other. He chattered, but I didn't hear much of what he said, partly because of my octogenarian ears and partly because I was planning my escape. How silly I was. It was broad daylight. There were people around. But, I thought with relief, I could take refuge at Carol's place.

At the bottom of the steps, I turned left. He turned left. I felt my body tense. Then he asked, "Who is your favorite poet?" At a younger age I might have thought what a come-on. Instead, with some enthusiasm, I told him, "Kahlil Gibran." His voice was deep and rich as he recited these words I love:

> "And let your best be for your friend.
> If he must know the ebb of your tide, let him know its flood also.
> For what is your friend that you should seek him with hours to kill?
> Seek him always with hours to live.
> For it is his to fill your need, but not your emptiness.
> And in the sweetness of friendship, let there be laughter, and sharing of pleasures.
> For in the dew of little things the heart finds its meaning and is refreshed."

Without another word, he turned to go to La Taqueria. I walked on home filled with the joy of my life in Sebastopol.

THOUGHTS ABOUT DYING

Dear Family, Dear Friends,

Sunshine streams into my kitchen. The whiteness of the blossoms on my orchid plant becomes unbelievably, almost unbearably whiter. The hummingbird at the feeder hanging just outside the window dazzles me with the brilliance of its sundrenched feathers. Jackson lies on his back on the patio table, vulnerable, his body stretched as only a feline's can be, absorbing the sun into every pore.

It's a perfect day, I think, to share with you my thoughts on my approaching, inevitable death. Although my death is not imminent (as far as I know), it will come and I'd like you to know a bit about what's in my head and heart.

One's beliefs about an afterlife, I think, affect one's attitude toward death. So I will tell you what I believe.

First, I do not believe in a physical heaven or hell. I agree with Bradford Smith who writes (in pre-feminist language): "The teaching of a physical heaven in the skies is one of the worst stumbling blocks of religion, since it comes to us from a pre-scientific era, is stubbornly maintained by established churches, and is unacceptable to any thinking man...Heaven is not a physical place which an astronaut may someday reach; it is a state of mind to which any man may come, or at least aspire."

As for my soul, it's already commingled with Bob's. We were soul mates from the first. A pleasant surprise in these last six years since his death is the perfect sense that he is an inextricable part of me; I am part Bob. I do believe, as my mother taught me, that death is a part of life. I believe in a continuum of life, which I don't fully understand, but which I think is nonetheless valid.

Like Bob, whose body was given to the medical school at the University of San Francisco, I would like for my body, if accepted, to be used for some similarly useful purpose.

Like everyone else, I hope that I can end my life being little burden to my family and society. Burden has hidden meanings. I think of Pat who cared for our mother for several years after Mother fell and, due to cancer, could never walk again. That was a physical and financial burden for Pat, but her own assessment was that it was a privilege. "I saw Mother in a new light, as a whole person, one able to accept help with grace, not just the nurturer I'd always known." If I'm put in the spot to be a burden, I'll remember Mother and try to be as light a one as I can.

"Death is a part of life." A knowing good enough for my mother is an inspiration for me. Mother is my role model—for living and for dying.

In rummaging through some old files the other day, I found notes I had written following a medical appointment with Dr. Zweig in April, 1999, a couple of months after Bob died. Upon checking my heart and lungs, the doctor predicted I would live to be at least ninety-two. At that time, ninety-two was too far away to imagine. Now, it's closer by six years. Is that too close for comfort?

"You're not old until you're 100." Granddaughter Clare has told me that for years. Do I really want to get old, to live to be 100? When will I be ready to die?

I believe this is an honest statement: I am ready now...anytime is okay.

I've had a full life and I do not fear death. However, I intend to be fully involved in living until that time comes.

I would not want my life prolonged if dementia or Alzheimer's prevents me from making sense. As far as I know, there's no history of that in my family. But two of my siblings died unexpectedly in their sleep.

If I should die before I wake, please understand that's my preference. I've given this some thought: I know it would be a shock to survivors: that's a negative. Another negative is that I would miss the experience my own dying. Mary died in her sleep. She was found in bed with an unfinished crossword puzzle in her hand. Knowing my sister's desire to achieve, she probably was annoyed that she didn't get to finish the crossword; and, with her bright and curious mind, I think she would have liked to observe the miracle of her own death. (And who knows? Perhaps she did.) Positives about a sudden death in one's sleep are: less suffering from pain, less burden to others, and less expense. It seems more practical, but will I get a choice?

I wouldn't want to die in my sleep—or in any other way—until I get some tasks accomplished...like identifying the people in all those old snapshots, sorting out those boxes in storage, verifying arrangements with Redwood Funeral Society for proper delivery of my body to the University of San Francisco Medical School...that sort of thing. But I don't want to live like Helen, brother Dub's first wife, who kept the parsonage in "dying condition." She processed one load of laundry to completion, every item washed, folded or ironed, and put away, before she started another; no dishes left unwashed from one meal to the next; no last month's magazines on the coffee table. If I endeavored to live that way, I would surely succumb to a premature death.If, by any chance, I lose my will to live, I do not ask that you assist in my dying. I have already given written advice to Dr. Morse about when to withhold medical treatment. When I, of my own free will, decide I want to die, I would like to follow the example of Janet Nolan. Janet, in her nineties, ailing, asked that her caregivers honor her request for no medicine and no food. She soon died peacefully, and with dignity. If you are with me toward the end of my life, please honor such a request from me. You'd know for sure—if I decide to give up eating, I'm really ready to go.

Today is my 85th birthday. I resolve on this first day of the rest of my life to take care of my physical, mental, and spiritual health as best I can, to be mindful of the wonders that surround me, to be useful, and to love unconditionally.

I have been blessed, beyond reason, with the gifts of life and love. I am grateful for each day, but whenever death comes, don't grieve for me. Just mention my name once in a while...in token of the continuum of life.

Much love to each of you,

# PART FOUR: ON POLITICS

LETTER TO PRESIDENTIAL CANDIDATE JOHN KERRY

July 6, 2004

Dear Senator Kerry,

If this letter serves simply for a tally sheet, you can check me off as a definite vote FOR you for president. However, I qualify that with: I'm going to vote for you, BUT...

How I wish I felt like putting up a Kerry sign in my yard, a bumper sticker on my car, and sending a check bigger than I can afford! What can you do to make me enthusiastic about supporting you?

The issue of PEACE is my #1 issue—peace being more than the absence of war.

What bold, concrete plan do you have for building peace for the long term? What can you do to change the "bring 'em on" philosophy embraced by so many ordinary, well-meaning, patriotic citizens? How will you honor the peaceniks? What plan do you have to harness their terrific energy to protest war and warmongering and put that energy into peace-building activities? How can your presidency glorify the miracle of a country–and a world–getting along, learning patience for peace? How can you deglamorize attitudes that promote war?

What specific emphasis will your administration give to peace...to research, experimentation, study, practice, and glorification of solving problems without war, without violence? Would you expand the Peace Corps? Would you establish a Department of Peace with sufficient influence and budget to make it significant? What do you propose?

I will look for your answers to my concern in your issues statements and in the news. I want to be your ardent supporter.

Sincerely,
Dorothy Hansen

DIFFERENT PERSPECTIVES

Last Saturday night, November 13, 2004, the Sonoma County Peace and Justice Center held its 20th Anniversary dinner at the Veterans Memorial Building in Sebastopol, California. More than 300 members and friends packed the auditorium where tables were attractively set to serve a festive dinner prepared entirely with organic foods. Before dinner, no-host drinks were available in another large room where hundreds of items were displayed for purchase at a silent auction.

On November 2nd, George W. Bush was re-elected president of the United States, much to the disappointment and despair of the Peace and Justice Center. It has been active every day for over twenty years teaching peace. George Bush's agenda is a continuation of the preemptive war he imposed on Iraq and a promise of unilateral military aggression to "wipe terror off the face of the earth." The mood of the event could have been gloomy. Instead there was an atmosphere of confidence, of solidarity—friends greeting friends with hugs and hellos, easy talk among newcomers and old-timers—and hope that good will come from their work.

The talking, the laughter, the shoddy acoustics of the Veterans Building required people to talk and laugh louder and louder to be heard. It was noisy! It was a test of commitment to stay for the program.

Instead of having one speaker relate the twenty year history of the Peace and Justice Center, three of the founding members—Adrienne Swenson, Lucy Forrest, and George Romandy—were on stage, with long-time member Earl Herr to facilitate their conversation about its past. I strained to hear what they had to say as my husband and I had been members since its early days. Something George Romandy said sparked a memory.

After a four-year absence Bob and I returned to Sonoma County in the early 1980s. We quickly connected with the antiwar group that had continued after the Vietnam war to be a permanent presence in the community to promote peace and justice. Although our time was consumed with running our business and active participation in the Cotati food cooperative, we supported the peace group as best we could. We kept informed by reading its lively, informative newsletter.

The newsletter, however, was mimeographed. Compared to the printing we did on the offset printer we used for our business, their newsletter looked out-of-date and was often hard to read. Bob and I had an idea: to print their newsletter for them. First, we had to talk it over with Ted Young, our twenty-something employee who did our printing. Ted was a self-taught printer who learned the trade when we bought an A.B. Dick Offset printer to do our business printing in-house. We knew little about Ted's politics. We needed to know from him if he had any political or other objection to printing the peace group's newsletter. We explained something of their philosophy about war, their opposition to nuclear power and nuclear weapons, their public activism in marching and civil disobedience and resistance to military service. Ted was a quiet, rather shy young man, but there was no hesitancy in his answer. "I'd be proud to print it," he said. Now, we were set to make the offer to the peace center.

George's reminiscences of that offer are from a different perspective. He spoke of the early days when the peace center was struggling. The intense interest and involvement during the Vietnam war had diminished, yet there was a determined group that believed having a strong, viable peace network in the community was a goal worth pursuing. He remembered one meeting where only he and Adrienne were present. They waited and waited for others to come. After a while, they were so discouraged they talked of abandoning the whole project, and then, he said, "Bob and Dorothy Hansen showed up." He described our offer in detail and gave us credit for keeping their hope alive. Bob, who died six years ago, would have been as surprised as I to learn how timely our offer was.

Although I don't remember the story as George told it, somehow I can close my eyes and believe it. Bob and I didn't know the group was near despair: our thought was simply to make a contribution that we knew we could do well. I can visualize its being a dark winter's night, raining a little. Bob and I are holding hands, walking up the steps to an old house on College Avenue, going into a dimly lit room. I can almost believe I remember. Sometime I'll ask George about it.

They accepted our offer. It was a pleasure for us, and for Ted, to print the Peace and Justice Center newsletter for several years. When the time came that we could no longer provide that support, I fretted for weeks trying to devise an alternative plan. What would they do without us?

What they did was to find new printers—Paz printing collective—and enlarge, expand and improve the newsletter...and now, to celebrate the 20th Anniversary of the Sonoma County Peace and Justice Center.

♭

ABU GHRAIB

All I can do is pray
You said
I tried to jest
To which god will you pray?
Bin Laden's?
Sharon's?
To the god who called George W. Bush to be president?

My jest fell flat

Of course you can
You must pray
Who denies the power of prayer?

But is that all you can do?
You—who awakens in a soft, clean bed
Who bathes in water the temperature of your choosing
Who lives in a house with a flushing toilet.

You—well-educated, hard-working, generous, kind
How can prayer be all you offer?

Does your prayer give you courage?
Courage to speak up now when your voice
Might tip the scales toward justice
Courage to wear something red each Friday
To identify yourself with the peacemakers

Yes, my friend, pray
Pray for strength
Strength and wisdom
To be more skilled at peacemaking
Than the warmongers are at killing

Pray. Let prayer be your comfort
And a jumpstart to acts of loving kindness
To a passion and patience for peace

LETTER TO AN ELDERLY IRAQI WIDOW

Dear Friend,

This letter is being delivered to you by a peacemaker, Martin Edwards, who lives in a town about fifteen miles from Sebastopol, California, United States of America, which is where I live. I am very proud that our city council approved a resolution urging our federal government to use peaceful methods in resolving the conflict with your country. One hundred other cities in the United States have passed similar resolutions. One of our council members, Sam Spooner—along with representatives from twenty-five of those cities—recently went to Washington, D.C. hoping to deliver the resolution in person to President Bush. Enclosed is a clipping from our local newspaper about his trip.

I am grateful that Martin Edwards' visit to Iraq allows me the opportunity to send this letter directly to you. Martin is in Iraq as a volunteer with the Peace Team project of Voices in the Wilderness. He travels in jeopardy as, by visiting Iraq as a member of the Peace Team, he is committing an act of civil disobedience and is under threat of imprisonment and large fines by our government. He feels called to bear witness for peace, and, in addition to the medicine he brings, he carries letters from America to let you know that many, many, many of us do care about you and about what happens to you.

Both Martin Edwards and I are members of the Religious Society of Friends (also known as Quakers). Quakers believe there is something of the Divine within every person. We are opposed to war, of course, but we are also called to be active advocates for peace. For more than 300 years, Quakers have worked with both sides to bring understanding and reconciliation toward a peaceful resolution of a conflict.

I am an eighty-three-year-old widow. I have many happy, comforting memories as I lived fifty years with a fine husband. He died four years ago. My husband refused to be a soldier in World War II and served as a conscientious objector for several years as an aide in the violent ward of a mental hospital.

Now I try to do what I can for peace, in my place of worship, and with a group of Women in Black who vigil for an hour each Friday at noon on the main intersection in our town. We dress in black and silently grieve for all the victims of violence. There are Women in Black in many countries, so we stand with all of them in solidarity against war and violence.

My aging arthritic knees prevented me from making the long march for peace on Sunday, February 16, in San Francisco, but I was privileged to attend the rally with son Tom, his wife Robyn and their friend Christine where I heard many speeches from all segments of society.

There were thousands and thousands of people there, and it was very inspiring to me to be with so many people speaking out for peace.

Although I do not know your circumstances and how the sanctions, the "no fly zone" bombings, and the threats of all-out war affect you and your family, I hope and pray that you are safe and will soon be able to live a life free of fear.

In Friendship,

Dorothy Hansen

♄

Tom, Robyn, Dorothy, Christine, San Francisco Peace March 2003

HARD WORK

Below are listed excerpts from a transcript of the first debate between the candidates for the presidency of the United States, President George W. Bush and Senator John F. Kerry, held at the University of Miami, Coral Gables, Florida, on Thursday, September 30, 2004: (MT = my thoughts)

    Bush: "It's hard work. It's incredibly hard."
    Bush: "There's a lot of good people working hard."
    Bush: "There's a lot of really good people working hard."
    Bush: "It's hard work."
    Bush: "And it's hard work. I understand how hard it is."
    Bush: "It is hard work."
    Bush: "It's hard work."
    Bush: "You know. It's hard work..."
    Bush: "We've done a lot of hard work..."

MT: What a shame you've had to work so hard. You deserve a long rest—retirement, really. Go back to Texas. Just relax at your ranch. Rest. Don't do a thing—that's the best contribution you can make. The whole world will love you for that. Rest in peace.

♄

HEY, HEY, HO, HO, WTO HAS GOT TO GO

An Open Letter to the Editor of Friends Bulletin

[Note: I included this letter in the Apple Core, newsletter of Apple Seed Meeting of the Religious Society of Friends (Quakers) which I prepare each month. A copy of the Jack Powelson article was inserted in the newsletter. For lack of space, I did not make complete quotes from the article.]

It is with some misgivings that I enclose two dollars for a free copy of Jack Powelson's book, Seeking Truth Together. I found his "Hey, Hey..." article rather disturbing and hope that a reading of the complete book will help me understand his thinking. The author's use, in the very first paragraph, of an inflammatory quote from the Wall Street Journal didn't get the article off to a good start for me.

In your editor's column, you say "Jack Powelson is convinced that, ultimately, the free market will bring about empowerment and prosperity for everyone, including the poor."

What about the free market where fast food companies destroy rain forests, oppose raising the minimum wage, receive government subsidies for "training" employees (for what?), and is delighted that employees, on average, last about three months permitting the companies to pay no benefits, cut their payroll costs, and please their stockholders with their "efficiency"? (Fast Food Nation by Eric Schlosser)

...Or the free market where scofflaw executives of Archer Daniels Midland Company conspire with their foreign competitors to fix prices and allocate market share, meanwhile portraying themselves on public television as benefactors to the world? (The Informant by Kurt Eichenwald)

...Or the free market where the privatized prison corporations effectively lobby for laws that are "tough on crime" so the cells of their supermax prisons will be kept full and profitable for their corporate executives and shareholders? (Going Up the River by Joseph Hallinan)

With our free market nation fast becoming America, Inc., I am keen to know how the author sees a market economy as the solution.

LETTER TO THE IRS

Via Certified Mail
Reference: Notice Number CP518
Notice Date: 2005-08-01
Internal Revenue Service
Tax Period: 200312
Ogden, UT 84201-0030

August 4, 2005

Dear IRS:

In response to your communication referenced above, I regret that I cannot comply. My faith and my conscience do not allow me to be complicit in the killing of my fellow human beings.

It is wrong to kill. I learned that as a child in Methodist Sunday school. My parents set a good example for our big family by teaching us cooperation and showing us love.

I am now 85 years old and have paid taxes for over 60 years. Although my late husband was a conscientious objector in World War II, we paid taxes. As a widow I continued to pay taxes. Each year I struggled for the strength to be a war tax resister. As a pacifist, and now as a Quaker, I can no longer pay for war. My Quaker faith helped me find the courage to be true to my convictions.

It was our government's shameful, unwarranted, illegal, unprovoked war on Iraq that compelled me to express my utter condemnation of such flagrant killing.

As a citizen, it is my right and duty to peacefully protest the actions of our government when I believe it to be taking a wrong course. The strongest peaceful protest I can make is to withdraw from the tax system that forces me to comply with actions that I cannot accept, actions that go against my faith and my conscience.

While I will not advise other taxpayers to take the action I have taken—it is much too personal a decision—I hope my experience will help others know there are options to explore.

But I will vigorously encourage everyone to support the National Campaign for a Peace Tax Fund. I would gladly pay taxes if there were a Peace Tax Fund which would assure me, as a sincere conscientious objector, that none of my taxes would go for war.

I cannot bear to have more lives taken in my name. I grieve with families in our country, in Afghanistan and Iraq, in Haiti and wherever in the world we have imposed our will with force.

I cry with those who wonder why their loved ones are dead or crippled or no longer themselves. I am ashamed that my tax dollars have, even in the smallest way, helped cause those deaths and injuries and such awful sadness.

War is not the answer. As privileged Americans, we can use our talents and our treasure to find a better way.

"To thine own self be true." This is the richest legacy I can give my family—that I have stood up for what I believe.

I ask for your understanding.

Sincerely,
Dorothy L Hansen

cc: Senators Boxer and Feinstein
Representative Woolsey
The Press Democrat
The North Bay Progressive
Now Democracy
The National Campaign for a Peace Tax Fund
AFSC
KPFA
KSRO
NWTRCC
FCNL

TAX POLICY AND THE UNION HOTEL

Last night Bob and I took Susan and Bert to the Union Hotel in Occidental for dinner. There was only one family and one lone male diner in a booth near us in the dining room. Bob talked about his idea of leaving his estate to the government upon death in lieu of paying income taxes. A lively, back and forth exchange interspersed with lots of laughter continued for the duration of our meal. As the lone diner was leaving, he stopped at our table to tell us how much he had enjoyed our conversation.

Bert and Sue, circa 1994

NOTICE OF DEFICIENCY

I've waited a long time for the other shoe to drop. I wondered how I would react. When the postman rang my doorbell, I could see he held a letter from the Internal Revenue Service. "I know what that's about," I said. "An audit," he suggested. "No, not that," I said while signing for the letter. "I am a war tax resister," I said proudly. He wasn't my regular postman: he didn't know what a war tax resister was, and cared even less. I couldn't share this important moment with him.

Now, the IRS meant business: this NOTICE OF DEFICIENCY is the beginning of a formal process to collect my withheld taxes. The letter was dated April 14, 2008. It was April 15, 2003, that I did not file my federal income taxes. For the first time I committed an act of civil disobedience. I took it seriously: I had always paid taxes and felt privileged to do my part. I had prepared my tax return but I could not sign it. My hand would not do the dirty work; my heart said: Don't pay for killing. I followed my heart, and have not filed an income tax return since.

My first communication from the IRS was a letter dated August 1, 2005, and since then we have carried on a correspondence; that is, until May of 2006 when they said my reasons for not paying were "frivolous" and that they did not want any more "frivolous" correspondence. I complied by not answering that or subsequent letters.

There is a deadline of July 15, 2008. I have to decide before that time if I want to protest. Ordinarily, I could go to the Appeals Office of IRS, but unfortunately, they don't consider cases involving moral, religious, political, constitutional, conscientious, or similar grounds. I can go to the United States Tax Court, but if they determine that my case is "frivolous" they can award up to $25,000 to the United States.

What to do? I'm not whining about my predicament. I'm not blaming anyone else for these worrisome days. I went against the law for the most non-frivolous reason I can think of, and I feel good about that. I asked for my trouble, but...

Why hasn't the Congress passed H. R. 1921? It would solve my problems and those of hundreds (or thousands) of war tax resisters who want to pay their taxes but can't for reasons of faith and conscience. H.R. 1921 affirms the religious freedom of taxpayers who are conscientiously opposed to participation in war by providing that the income, estate, or gift tax payments be used for nonmilitary purposes; it creates the Religious Freedom Peace Tax Fund to receive such payments.

Conscientious objection to participation in war in any form is recognized in Federal law with provision for alternative civilian service in lieu of military service by the Selective Training and Service Act of 1940; H.R. 1921 applies this to taxpayers. The Joint Committee on Taxation has certified that a tax trust fund would increase Federal revenues. If this were law, I, and other tax resisters, could pay all of our taxes into the Peace Tax Fund and the government would benefit as well.

Why doesn't this horrid war end? I had no intention of withholding taxes for such a long time. I am not only willing, but eager, to pay taxes — but not for war.

Refusing to pay taxes for war is serious business. Conscientious objectors have no status in the federal tax laws. The anti-war taxpayer must choose to go against his conscience and pay the taxes, or, go against the law by withholding all or part of the taxes due. If a taxpayer decides to withhold taxes, interest piles up on unpaid taxes; the IRS can add penalties, can confiscate property, raid bank accounts and other assets, even take a portion of social security payments, to collect the taxes withheld. In rare cases, war tax resisters have gone to jail. Even so, hundreds, if not thousands, of taxpayers choose to take the risk by following the road of conscience. I am glad to have joined their ranks.

♄

WHY I DIDN'T FILE A 2002 TAX RETURN

It took a rambunctious Oklahoma style thunderstorm for me, at age 83, to commit my first act of civil disobedience. Storms like that are not common where I live in Sebastopol, California, but one last winter changed my life. On that night, an enormous clap of thunder shattered my sleep while a flash of lightning filled my bedroom with an unreal brightness. Startled, I sat upright in bed and proclaimed, "I will not pay taxes for war anymore."

An epiphany? A spirit-led calling? Or just a bizarre experience? I felt great comfort and relief to be rid of the hypocrisy of paying taxes for killing when my conscience told me it was wrong. As a child, at home and at McFarlin Memorial Methodist Church in Norman, Oklahoma, I learned it was wrong to kill. How could I know that and pay for killing? At the beginning of World War II, I deliberately crossed the street to avoid greeting a longtime friend who was a conscientious objector. I was ashamed to let him know I worked at Tinker Air Force Base in Oklahoma City. Bob Hansen, another conscientious objector whom I met and married after the war, served on the violent ward of a Connecticut hospital for the mentally ill while I worked at the Pentagon. He was a strong man, true to his convictions, while I felt that I was only a fair weather pacifist.

In the fifty years of our marriage, Bob and I shared a desire to work for the common good, to do our bit toward a more equitable society. We rarely marched in protest but spent our energy supporting peace-building organizations, particularly consumer cooperatives. We dutifully paid federal taxes. How else can the government function if citizens don't pay taxes? We considered withholding the military portion of our taxes but concluded it was an ineffective way to work for peace. Our logic: The government eventually collects, adding interest and penalties to the amount not paid. By withholding, you pay more to the military than if you had paid in the first place. We did not withhold. There is no conscientious objector status for taxpayers.

Since Bob's death, I continued to pay taxes until my big decision struck last winter. Bolstered by my Quaker faith and Bob's celestial approval, I was determined not to pay taxes for war anymore. I considered my options: to withhold a symbolic $10.40 accompanied by a note of protest; to withhold an amount proportionate to the percentage of the federal budget that goes to the military; to file but not pay; or not to file at all.. Not to file carries the heaviest penalties. A lifelong procrastinator, I waited until the last minute to decide.

On April 15, 2003, I reviewed my tax calculations, opened my checkbook, clicked my pen, and sat at my desk, unable to write. My thoughts went to the millions of people around the world crying out for patience and compassion, protesting our country's invasion of Iraq; to the Bush administration's arrogant condescension toward the United Nations; to the harsh conservatives in this administration and in Congress who bring us unilateral, preemptive war without end. I thought of the soldiers who die and are maimed and who take the lives and limbs of innocent others for this administration's visions of empire—visions that distort and demean the meaning and purpose of these United States of America. There is no way to sort out the costs of war as they now permeate all aspects of our lives. I could not—and did not—file a tax return for 2002.

What risks have I taken for my new moral courage? The penalty for not filing can be severe. Since my income is small and my possessions few, the risk might be only interest plus a penalty; that is, if I pay when the Internal Revenue Service demands it. If I refuse to pay, the IRS may seize my bank account, my house (if I owned one), or my car (a Nissan Maxima with 220,000 miles on it). The worst punishment, I believe, is that I could go to jail. It's some comfort to know that in all the years of war tax resistance, less than three dozen people have been incarcerated.

However, with the neocons in the White House, the doormats in Congress, and Patriot Act II on its way (albeit in unnoticeable driblets attached to other legislation), could I somehow be accused of being a domestic terrorist? Or wind up at Guantanamo Bay? Some say, for an activist, going to jail is climbing a rung on the ladder to heaven. Will I be such a hero? Or will I melt down at the first sight of an IRS ID card?

Actor Martin Sheen, arrested and jailed for good causes more times than I've paid taxes, stated in a recent interview, "I honestly do not know if civil disobedience has any effect on the government. I can promise you it has a great effect on the person who chooses to do it." That is true. My life has changed. It's a great feeling to do what I know is right for me. I will work, pray, and pay for peace.

"To thine own self be true." For me, it took a while.

♮

WHAT WILL I DO?

The election is over. The Democrats lost. Self-appointed pundits palaver 24/7 with their pseudo-wisdom about what will happen these next four years. The world now knows Americans prefer having a beer with the imperial George W. Bush than with the less pre-emptive John Kerry.

Claiming a mandate, George W. Bush & Co. vows to spend the political capital he believes he has earned. Oblivious to the millions of saints and sinners who know war is not the answer, Bush is hell-bent to wipe out evil wherever he finds it and whatever he says it is. He hunkers over the lectern and tells us it's okay because of his "mandate" and his special connection to God.

The thing is, God has a special connection with a lot of people. God's audience is big, really huge. For as many years as there are, God has told all who listen that it's not good to kill each other. God suggests ways to avoid that.

Love thy neighbor. Do unto others as you would have them do unto you. Whatever faith one holds, whatever vision of God one has, whatever one thinks of the possibility of life everlasting, these truths are eternal.

Accepting these truths puts me in clear opposition to the Bush agenda. As a human being on this planet, as a woman, a Californian, a voter, as a Quaker and a pacifist, what am I going to do about it? As an 84-year-old, what can I do to ameliorate the suffering, the slaughter, promised for the next four years? How can I make a difference?

I have a plan in the making. First, I need to make time and space for action. Dawdling is out. Gandhi said there's "more to life than "increasing its speed,". Maybe I've taken that too much to heart. A little hustle might be what I need. Or maybe a helper to do some of those chores I used to take in stride. Now an ordinary task takes inordinate time to do the job, and also requires time to contemplate whether to do it at all. With my newfound efficiency will come time and zest for innovative and renewed endeavors...such as writing letters.

Letters of encouragement will be my specialty. Congresswoman Lynn Woolsey needs to know from me that I support her as she works in the House of Representatives to ward off the assaults on civil rights and the Constitution that can be expected to continue. I'll write Congressman Dennis Kucinich to support a cabinet-level Department of Peace.

My plan includes being more plainspoken. I'll read the upbeat book "Difficult Conversations" so I can engage people with different points of view (including my brother Hoyl) more constructively, listening to and learning from each other. I aim to be a better listener–especially if it's God that's speaking.

In 2005, for the third year I will continue to withhold federal income taxes to protest militarism. As a member of Sonoma County Taxes for Peace, I will become better informed so I can offer to others facts about the benefits and risks of war tax resistance.

When there's a move to impeach George W., count me in. Being a pacifist doesn't mean being passive.

Whatever else I do, I will hold everyone—terrorists and George Bush & Co. included—in the light, so that we do what's needed to live on this planet in peace. I will be reminded by the framed mantra on my wall: For things to change, I must change.

ђ

THE GIANT UMBRELLA

Watch out, world, I'm on a roll
I'm gonna wipe out Evil
Wherever it is
Whatever I say it is

('Scuse me
I meant to say we
You know, Jeb, and Cheney
Libby and Rumsfeld
And Wolfowitz
We been workin' on our
Project For A New Century
For longer than you'd guess)

I'm just warnin' everybody who's evil
Watch out for the US of A
We're sittin' on tons of those
Weapons of mass destruction.
And we ain't afraid to use 'em.
We done it before.

Trent Lott falls right in line
Atta boy, prez, you tell 'em
That's what I told that congressman
Over there in Baghdad
He said you just might be exaggeratin' a bit
About those Iraqis.
I told him right there on TV
Y'all just come back here and shut up.

Outrageous. Outrageous.
Thunders Tom Daschle
From the Senate floor
He's not in a tizzy

About starting another war
That's okay with him
He's just pissed that Bush
Maligned the Senate for stalling
Big Al Gore shakes up the
status quo
Oh, yeah, war is all right with him
That is, if it's done with grace.
You know, get the UN's approval
Grease it through the Congress
They love to think they have power.

Colin Powell, who knows that
War is Hell and Evil is in each of us
Wanders around the world
Touting a crusade so unholy
He must want to retch.
Yet he does not speak Truth to us.

Where are our moral leaders when we need them?
Did they die in World War II?
In Korea?
In Vietnam?

Where is the leader
who will remind us
Of what we profess to believe
That we must love our neighbors as ourselves.
That we must do good to those who harm us.
That we must do unto others as we would have them do unto us.

Here we are
Well-educated, well-fed
Millions upon millions of Americans
Vainly going about our personal affairs
Denying the moral dilemma that
Demands our clearest thinking

Here we are,
Confident the Divine Spirit
Sparkles most brightly in our souls,
Millions upon millions of Americans

Supporting Evil for Evil with silence
Taking protection from sins of inaction
Under a giant, tattered Umbrella of Propaganda
Dare we hope
There will be one more than the millions needed
One more who will emerge from subservience
One more who refuses to be a victim of power and greed
One more who will not tolerate an Umbrella of Propaganda

Dare we hope
To see light through the umbrella's dirty fabric
To stop the crusade to force the world do our bidding
To choose leaders with the patience for peace
To do unto others as we would have them do unto us

I do so dare

— 2002

BUT WHAT DID I DO?

My oldest son John went to Nevada the weekend of October 4-5, 2008 to help get Barack Obama elected president. There were almost a thousand northern Californians who attended a class in their own community and then met in Reno for a weekend of voter registration and precinct work.

John came back with glowing reports of a well-organized, high-spirited event. They were welcomed at a Friday night gathering where their duties were outlined specifically and appropriate materials given them for the tasks to be done—voter registration forms, nametags...and assignments taken for specific places to work. The local Democrats had prepared a potluck supper for a warehouse full of people; he said there must have been eight or nine tables seating ten or twelve to a table. The next day was to canvass the precincts. The materials given to each participant showed the names of Democrats and Independents who had been seen before, and those that had been missed. It transcended the usual precinct work by being so well-prepared and with such good spirit. The local organizers also wanted people to know they had a ride to the polls on November 4th.

My landlord, who lives in Oakland, said he wanted to go to Reno, but they didn't need him. Instead, he'll show up in another battleground state, Florida, in time to help there. "Orlando, here I come." His wife is working at the Obama headquarters in Oakland every day, and his ex-wife is coordinator for the county wherever she lives.

Meanwhile, my youngest son and his wife in Kansas City, Missouri, were entertaining a guest. The guest was an Obama worker. The first one stayed for two weeks, and the second has been there for the past three months or so. She's going back home after the election is over. It's a commitment that would be hard for some to make, but they have a house that lends itself to sharing with others. Paul and Catherine also do precinct work.

My middle son Tom and his wife Robyn, were slow to come around to Obama with concerns that he would be no match for the political machinery and shenanigans of Capital Hill....but they finally came around. What did I do? I've read every article, heard every speech, bitten every nail. I am a nervous wreck. I don't believe the polls: today Obama's the winner by ten points. What will he be three weeks from now?

Anxious as I am about the election, even if Obama wins I will be like Howard Zinn, author of *A People's History of the United States* and *A Power Governments*

Cannot Suppress, who said, yes, he would vote for Obama but then "use whatever energy I have to push him toward a recognition that he must defy the traditional thinkers and corporate interests surrounding him, and pay homage to the millions of Americans who want real change."

♮

PART FIVE: POETRY

Dorothy, standing with Women in Black.
Main Street, Sebastopol, CA. 2004
Reprinted with permission from Northbay Bohemian.

A WOMAN IN BLACK

One hour one day a week
I stand in silent vigil
On the corner of Main and Bodega
In Sebastopol, California
Dressed in black
The symbol of mourning

I stand in solidarity
With women around the world
Who also stand
One hour one day a week
To publicly share our grief
For victims of violence

The placard that I carry
Says we grieve for all
The victims of violence
"All" is underlined

I grieve for the victims of
The dastardly acts of 9/11
I grieve for the victims of
Our own country's relentless
Bombing in Afghanistan
For victims of our arrogance
And our unquenchable thirst for power
I grieve for victims of
Rape, torture, and death.
I grieve for the victims
Of personal rage or insanity

Of cult terrorism
Of corporate greed and graft
Of national propaganda and deception
Of international tolerance that permits
There to be victims of violence

I grieve for those who think they are God
Who say we have no quarrel with the
People of Iraq
Yet vow to kill them in cold blood
With our smart bombs and
Dumb decisions

I will continue to stand
One hour one day each week
In public silent solidarity
Grieving for all the victims of violence
Even though I know too well
It is not enough

WELCOME, KILEY

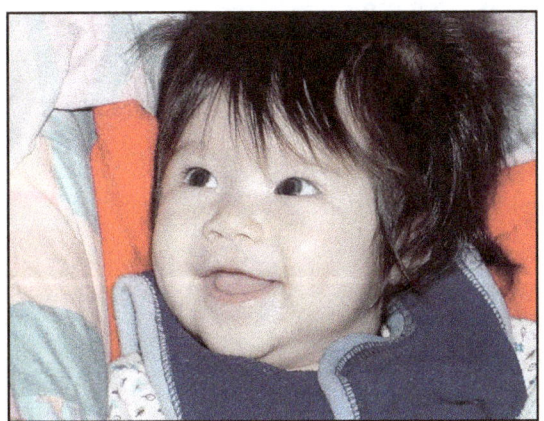

Kiley Lockett, 2001

When I was young I saw our family
as a large, loving cluster of
like-minded souls
all white
all Methodist
all Democrats

Barely mentioned but ingrained
were expectations of good grades, good grooming,
Sunday school, church, college
no smoking, no drinking, no swearing,
no sex.

Within a culture as flat as the Oklahoma plains
our pleasures came from family and friends
all white
all Methodist
all Democrats.

Unlike the plains with their vast, open horizons
our lives were—without our
really knowing —
confined within the framework
of tight social customs.

There was safety in that sameness
safety, security, assurance
but the soul demands stretching.
Things don't stay the same.

Look at us now. It's 2002. At eighty-two
I see broader horizons, a richer culture
in our once frame-bound family.

Welcome, baby Kiley
with your jet black hair, impish smile
the newest little one for us to love.
Within the warmth of this family
you will find more than Methodists.
Presbyterians. Quakers. Agnostics. Jews.
New Age followers of
unpronounceable gurus.
Some non-religious (of those quite a few)

A blending of races
Some Republicans
A wide range of lifestyles
Mom's, Pop's and kids, adopted or not
single parents, same-sex marriages, partners,
divorcees, singles, widowers and widows
all welcomed, all loved.

Philosophers, preachers, professors
seven PhDs, a postmaster
a physical therapist, a pilot
educators, engineers, an epidemiologist
A nuclear weapons disarmament negotiator

Inventors, a lawyer, financial consultants
musicians, manufacturers,
budding biologists

seamen, salesmen, a pet store staffer
carpenters, corporate execs, computer wonks
Devotees of car racing, the Grateful Dead,
quilt making, Scrabble.

Political activists, placard-bearing peaceniks
People with passion to reach out, to grow
A whole passel of people to love you.

If our family is a microcosm
of changes made and yet to come,
there is hope.

Welcome, Kiley, to this wonderful world!

THE MIDNIGHT CALLER

NOTE: This is a true incident in the life of my sister,
Susan Patty (Pat) Markley

There was an old lady
Who lived all alone.
For a sense of security
She slept near a phone.
She awakened one night
To the sound of a ringing;

She picked up the phone
and it stopped tingalinging.
She heard a male voice
But her hearing was weak
She asked, "To whom, sir,
Do you wish to speak?"

"Not to YOU, lady,"
Were the words that he said.
He slammed the receiver.
She went back to bed.

Now remember, dear ladies,
When you answer the phone
Just use proper grammar
And you'll be left alone.

FOR TEDDY

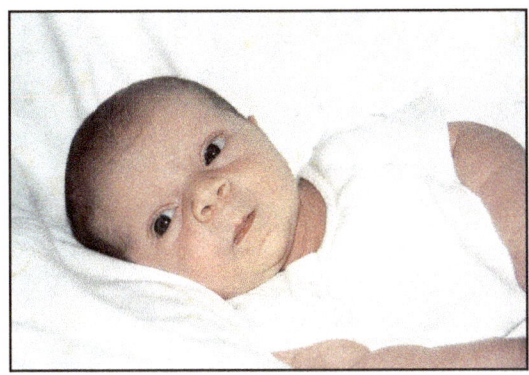

Theodore Lockett, 2001

Here's a furry friendly animal
With a soft and fuzzy tail.
(It's taken me a long time
To send it through the mail.)

I wish that you will like it.
You name it what you please.
When its tail is near your nose
I wonder if you'll sneeze!

It will tickle you and hug you,
Or wipe your tears away,
Snuggle up real close to you
'Til night turns into day.

This little brown bright-eyed thing
This fluffy little squirrel
Can be your special playmate
Your best friend in the world.

The squirrel asked me to tell you
Your hand goes in its pocket.
So now you are a two-some —
The squirrel and Teddy Lockett.

From Great-Aunt Dodo, 2002

ON AGING

I don't have a quarrel
With those seeking Suchness
If that's what they're looking for
That's what they'll get.

But
If I should seek Suchness
'T would seem a bit muchness
For whatever I'd find
I would promptly forget.

2003

A POLKA DOT PATH

Fallen pink petals from my plum tree
Form a polka-dot path to my door.
It's a fairyland sight.
I am filled with delight.
Pink polka-dot paths, je t'adore. Mi amor

2007

A BUMP ON THE HEAD

I looked for a book, a hardcover book
a book I had already read.
I found it up high; I reached to the sky.
I need to reread what it said.
The book slipped my grip; it took quite a trip
as it crashed kerplunk on my head.

I don't get the message.
It seems rather odd
to get whacked on the head
by the "Left Hand of God."

2007

BEACONS OF LIGHT AROUND THE WORLD

The sky sparkled. The moon shone brightly.
It was a night for Love.

About a quarter to seven
My neighbors Carol and Rhea and I
Walked together the few blocks to the
Downtown plaza in Sebastopol where
We joined several hundred other people
To participate in a world-wide
Candlelight Vigil for Peace.

I LOVE YOU, ROBYN

Do you remember, Robyn
That morning at the hospital
They had taken me to Palm Drive
A heart attack, I learned later
The family was gathered around
Saying their good-byes

And you whispered in my ear
I love you, Dorothy
And I responded with
an asinine, "Thank you."

Later, we laughed about it.
I didn't know what was going on
I was completely out of it
I could have said
I love you, Robyn
I love you for being so good to me
For being a perfect wife for Tom
For being the bright-eyed pixie that you are
Bringing fun and gaiety to everyday happenings

I could have said
I love you for remembering
I love yellow flowers
Yellow tea towels
And sunshine

So here's to love expressed
Talked about, mentioned
Love that's acknowledged
By seeing, knowing, caring
Love like I have for you, dear daughter-in-law.

THE REMINDER OF MY GOOD FORTUNE

It's almost nine a.m.
when the phone rings
"Are you up yet?" a cheerful voice asks.

"No, not yet. You know, Tom, I'm slow
to get up after I awaken.
I don't move at all the whole night through
I wake up in the very same position
In the morning my leg muscles are tight
And my arms feel dead
And my head aches.
I feel every one of my eighty-eight and
one-fourth years."

"Are you going to class today?"

"No, I don't think so.
I don't have anything written
I'll call Freya and tell her I'm not going
I don't have to go."

"Mom, you *get* to go to class."

And here I am
Thankful for the privilege and
The reminder of my good fortune.

2008

www.ingramcontent.com/pod-product-compliance
Lightning Source LLC
Chambersburg PA
CBHW081152290426
44108CB00018B/2521